SpringerBriefs in Law

SpringerBriefs present concise summaries of cutting-edge research and practical applications across a wide spectrum of fields. Featuring compact volumes of 50 to 125 pages, the series covers a range of content from professional to academic. Typical topics might include: • A timely report of state-of-the art analytical techniques • A bridge between new research results, as published in journal articles, and a contextual literature review • A snapshot of a hot or emerging topic • A presentation of core concepts that students must understand in order to make independent contributions SpringerBriefs in Law showcase emerging theory, empirical research, and practical application in Law from a global author community. SpringerBriefs are characterized by fast, global electronic dissemination, standard publishing contracts, standardized manuscript preparation and formatting guidelines, and expedited production schedules

More information about this series at http://www.springer.com/series/10164

Kenneth K. Mwenda

Doctoral Degree Programs in Law

An International and Comparative Study of the English-Speaking World

Springer

Kenneth K. Mwenda
The University of Pretoria
Pretoria, South Africa

The World Bank
Washington, DC, USA

ISSN 2192-855X ISSN 2192-8568 (electronic)
SpringerBriefs in Law
ISBN 978-3-030-88420-8 ISBN 978-3-030-88421-5 (eBook)
https://doi.org/10.1007/978-3-030-88421-5

This Springer imprint is published by the registered company Springer Nature Switzerland AG
The registered company address is: Gewerbestrasse 11, 6330 Cham, Switzerland

Foreword

The 40th UNESCO General Conference was convened in Paris from November 12 to 27, 2019. The conference focused on emerging initiatives in the education, science, culture and youth sectors. As the Minister of Higher Education for the Republic of Zambia, I was assigned by the Zambian Government to represent its interests on matters for consideration at that conference. I led a high-powered government delegation comprising senior technocrats from my Ministry, including the Permanent Secretary and Directors as well as the Chief Executive Officers of the Higher Education Authority (HEA) and the Zambia Qualifications Authority (ZAQA), the two institutions that serve as implementing agencies under the Ministry of Higher Education.

Of key interest to me, apart from the excitement of spending almost a month in Paris, were the issues of qualifications arising from key education initiatives. These initiatives included the Global Convention on the Recognition of Qualifications concerning Higher Education 2019 and the Qualifications Passport for Refugees and Vulnerable Migrants that was being piloted in Zambia. I was to report on these initiatives during and after the 40th UNESCO General Conference.

The initiatives, once we delved into them as the conference went on, covered further interesting details on the promotion of qualifications portability, standardization and recognition across jurisdictions and regions in a fair and equitable manner so as to give an opportunity to all, including refugees that have been displaced from their home countries, of accessing quality education.

Something that interested me quite abundantly, as a new Minister in charge of Higher Education in Zambia, was the idea of confronting some of the perceived obstacles around the internationalization of higher education and the issue of the portability of students' qualifications given the differences that existed in different education systems across different jurisdictions. I wanted to acquire new understanding, or attempted to understand the issue, of equitable and fair portability of qualifications where such portability did not inhibit or discourage free movement and sharing of knowledge. I knew that if qualifications from different regions were not understood well, or if qualifications frameworks were not compatible and to scale, then qualifications from one region might end up being ignored in another region. It would mean curtailing movements of people with some skills, trainings and qualifications once they felt that they could be sent to the back of a classroom and asked to start all over again if they were to move to another jurisdiction that did not recognize their qualifications fully or appropriately. This made me pay lots of attention to the deliberations and our submissions, as the conference progressed.

My delegation and I were perfectly aware that education systems and structures across different regions had some differences. It was therefore important to our delegation to follow the plans and initiatives that all member states were putting forward to address this obvious concern. The USA, for example, had a significantly different education progression structure compared to the UK, especially at collegiate level. And, the proposals from the conference called by UNESCO would be speaking to the convergence of these systems through thorough understanding of the various qualification frameworks and their intersections. For easy mobility of students from one region to the next, a clear understanding of levels of qualifications on the framework was extremely important so that entry into different education system were encouraged to happen at the right entrance levels.

Reflecting on the debates and the resolutions from that conference motivated me to agree to write this Foreword, as this book attempts to explore these differences, explaining the education and qualifications differences and offering opinions on each of the education systems under discussion. The different chapters of the book delve into the subject matter expertly on concepts of law and the issue of postgraduate training in law in the USA and the UK. The book further covers the concept of a higher doctorate (beyond the traditional JD or Ph.D. and yes, we thought the Ph.D. was the highest academic degree!) and goes further into the demands of each of those degrees, as per jurisdiction under discussion. This is a comprehensive and well-written book that shares timely and relevant information on distinctions and similarities, if any, in law qualifications across several regions. And, it could not have been written by a better author than Prof. Kenneth K. Mwenda, Ph.D., LL.D., D.Sc. (Econ.), an exceedingly intellectual and thought leader of our time who currently contributes his vast knowledge and competencies on the largest stage at the intersection of academia and geopolitics on the well-being of the world we live in. In writing this Foreword, it was an honor to partner with such a pleasant man and prolific writer, with presidential awards to his name.

As an international student at one point myself and having completed high school and pre-engineering courses in Zambia, I realized how different education systems could be firsthand as I transitioned from the UK-centric educational system to the USA. Knowing what I know now, it was not necessary to do certain courses before joining universities in the USA. This book helps people such as my former self-navigate the terrain while making sense of why some regions administer their educational systems and qualifications the way they do.

Please enjoy the book as it examines interesting topics and puts in context the education systems and qualifications at the highest levels. The topic on the concept of higher doctorate was very valuable to me as a policy maker in Zambia and I learnt a lot. I hope readers will reference the book in their furtherance of understanding of the different degrees and how those differences impact, for example, the duration of study or which degree demands the addition of new knowledge to the existing body of knowledge on the subject matter. With that understanding, potential students can truly make the best decisions as they seek fulfillment in attainment of further education anywhere in the world.

Lusaka, Zambia
March 2021

Eng. Brian C. Mushimba, Ph.D.
Minister of Higher Education,
Government of the Republic of Zambia

Preface

There is a dearth of literature on international and comparative studies of how law doctoral programs in much of the English-speaking world are structured. A chasm exists between the structure of law doctoral programs in the USA and UK. This book endeavors to fill that gap. The book aims at reconciling the structures of the American and British models of law doctorates. A related issue is the position of legal academia outside the USA and UK on how it regards US-styled doctorates and UK-styled doctorates. Indeed, are law schools in the English-speaking world outside the UK and the USA expected to grow their law doctoral programs along the lines of the American or British doctoral programs, given the disparity in the structure of law doctoral programs in the two countries?

It is a truism that many legal academics in Africa and Asia as well as in the Caribbean and Pacific countries continue to obtain law doctorates from the USA and the UK. Therefore, the influence of American and British legal education on other English-speaking countries cannot be downplayed. Indeed, should law schools in English-speaking world outside the USA and the UK adopt the US-styled Doctor of Juridical Science (JSD or SJD) or retain the UK-styled Ph.D. in Law? And how does legal academia in the English-speak world outside the USA and the UK view the Juris Doctor (JD), the JSD or SJD and the Ph.D. in Law degrees? Indeed, what are the pros and cons of each degree model as far as doctoral education is concerned? Is there something else beyond these degree programs that can help to reconcile the differences?

In this book, I have drawn extensively from my experiences at Harvard University and the University of Warwick, respectively, while carrying out studies there in matters of pedagogy and higher education teaching. Closely related to this, as I began to prepare for my higher doctorate degree in law in the mid-2000s, my intellectual curiosity in the varying structures of law doctoral programs in the USA and the UK grew. This interest benefitted additionally from my academic role as a Ph.D. supervisor and examiner at various leading universities. In 2008, I was admitted to the rarely awarded Higher Doctorate degree of Doctor of Laws (LL.D.) at Rhodes University following the examination of selected scholarly books and peer-refereed journal articles that I have authored. The LL.D. came almost ten (10) years after completing my Ph.D. in Law at the University of Warwick where I also served as Assistant Professor of Law at the time.

In 2014, following a similar process as in the LL.D., I was awarded a second Higher Doctorate degree, the Doctor of Science in Economics (D.Sc. (Econ.)), by the University of Hull. I hasten to add that I have examined the concept of a higher doctorate degree in Chap. 4 of this book. Here, suffice it to say that although I left full-time academia a few decades ago, I have maintained an active presence in academia. I have served as Extraordinary Professor of Law at the University of Pretoria in South Africa and have taught as Adjunct Professor of Law at American University Washington College of Law (WCL) in Washington DC, USA. I have also served as Visiting Full Professor of Law at a number of leading universities in Europe and South Africa, including the University of Miskolc in Hungary and the University of Cape Town (UCT). Further, I continue to serve concurrently as Extraordinary Professor of Law at the University of Lusaka, Zambia. I have also given lead lectures and presentations at major US universities, including Duke University, George Washington University, the University of Maryland, Temple University, Howard University and the University of South Florida. A number of my former law students have gone on to become judges of the Supreme Court, the Constitutional Court, the Court of Appeal and the High Court of their respective countries. Others have served as Attorney-General for their governments. There are also some of my former law students who are now law professors and prominent Cabinet Ministers in their respective countries.

Over the years, I have maintained a parallel academic and professional life, publishing academic books and other scholarly work in top journals and law reviews as well as holding various senior academic appointments at leading universities internationally, while serving with the World Bank. At the World Bank, I have served for a decade as Senior Counsel in the Legal Vice-Presidency, as well as Senior Counsel in the World Bank's Integrity Vice-Presidency, before taking up my current role as the Program Manager and Executive Head of the World Bank Voice Secondment Program (VSP). I have also been invited and interviewed, as a thought leader and public intellectual, by numerous print and broadcast media, including the *New York Times* (USA), the *Voice of America* (VOA, USA), *CCTV* (USA), the *Times* (UK), the *British Broadcasting Corporation* (BBC, UK), and *Sky TV* (UK). On Saturday, May 25, 2019, the President of the Republic of Zambia, H.E. President Dr. Edgar C. Lungu conferred on me the prestigious Presidential Insignia of Meritorious Achievement (PIMA), the nation's highest civilian honor for meritorious achievement. The PIMA award ranks as the equivalent of the US Presidential Medal of Freedom, and it was conferred on me in recognition of my distinguished scholarly achievements in the field of law, as evidenced by the extensive body of my scholarly publications. A few years before that, President Lungu's predecessor, H.E. Mr Rupiah Banda, through his Minister of Tourism, conferred on me the lifetime achievement award of Honorary Tourism Ambassador for the Republic of Zambia, in recognition of my distinguished thought leadership and scholarship.

In a work of this kind, I am mindful that I owe my gratitude to many people. Indeed, it is not without difficulty that I record my indebtedness to all the people that I owe my gratitude. If I omit or forget to mention anyone, please forgive me.

Let me start by thanking the good Lord, God Jehovah Almighty, and my dearest parents, Mr. Joseph T. Mwenda and Mrs. Esther M. Mwenda. To God, our Father, His mercy endures forever. The fear of the Lord is the beginning of wisdom. To my dearest parents, though you have crossed over, your fatherly and motherly love endures forever. Your words of wisdom will forever remain indelible in my heart, edifying my thoughts and aspirations. I thank you for everything.

I am also exceedingly humbled and most grateful to my good brother, the Honorable Minister of Higher Education for the Republic of Zambia, Dr. Brian C. Mushimba, an astute scholar and thought leader, for honoring this book with a Foreword. There can be no greater honor in a treatise of this kind, that is, a book on higher education, than having the Foreword written by the Minister of Higher Education. For, he deals with what the book is all about on a daily basis. Dr Mushimba, a Ph.D. holder, with a background in mining engineering, is also a member of parliament in the Republic of Zambia. Thus, he stands at the frontiers of global policy on higher education. Indeed, he has not only walked the path of higher education as a scholar and development practitioner but has also dealt with higher education from the rare heights of a senior government official responsible for formulating and implementing higher education policies in Zambia. And so, I am eternally grateful to Dr. Mushimba for lending his voice to my scholarly work.

On the home front, my lovely wife, Dr. Judith Mvula-Mwenda, and my adorable son, Joseph, have been my rock. I cannot thank them enough. I am grateful for their patience, understanding and support, as I worked tirelessly long hours in the night and on weekends to bring this book to fruition.

Further, I would be remiss if I did not acknowledge the meticulous research support of my dear wife, Dr. Mvula-Mwenda, together with the editorial assistance of my good learned friend, Mr. Mwangala Simataa, at Georgetown University Law Center in Washington DC. That said, the interpretations and conclusions expressed in this book are entirely those of the author. They do not necessarily represent the views of the World Bank, its executive directors or the countries they represent. All the facts and the law presented in this book are as at the date of publication of the book.

Washington, DC, USA
September 2021

Kenneth K. Mwenda, Ph.D., LL.D., D.Sc. (Econ.)

Contents

List of Figures

Chapter 1
Introduction

Abstract This Chapter is the introduction of the study and sets forth the key research questions as well as the underlying thesis. A key objective of the study, as spelt out in this chapter, is to provide an international and comparative analysis of the efficacy of the American and British-styled models of law doctorates. Although there are various types of doctoral awards, the book focusses mainly on law doctorates, not doctoral awards conferred outside the field of law. That the structure of doctoral degree programs in law differ between the United States (US) and much of the Commonwealth is an issue that requires no contest. What is missing, however, as this chapter contends, is a narrative on how these programs are structured and how they compare. This book attempts to fill that gap.

Keywords Doctorate · Doctoral awards · Doctoral degree programs · Doctor of Juridical Sciences (SJD/JSD) · Juris Doctor (JD) · Doctor of Philosophy (Ph.D.) · Professional doctorates · Law doctorates · Post-JD · Master of Laws (LLM) · Foreign-trained lawyers · American Bar Association (ABA) · Recognition of qualifications · World-class doctoral program · Higher doctorate

1.1 What is a Doctorate?

That the structure of doctoral degree programs in law differ between the United States (US) and much of the Commonwealth is an issue that requires no contest. What is missing in the discourse, however, is a narrative on how these programs are structured and how they compare. This book attempts to fill that gap. A key objective of the study is to provide an international and comparative analysis of the efficacy of the American and British-styled models of law doctorates. At the outset, it is important to stress that although there are various types of doctoral awards, the book focusses mainly on law doctorates, not doctoral awards conferred outside the field of law. Examples of doctoral awards not commonly found in the field of law in the United Kingdom and many parts of the Commonwealth include professional doctorates and integrated doctorates. By contrast, in the US, the first professional law degree, the Juris Doctor (JD), is often considered as a professional doctorate. Also, as we shall see in Chap. 3, the post-JD American-styled Doctor of Juridical

K. K. Mwenda, *Doctoral Degree Programs in Law*,
SpringerBriefs in Law, https://doi.org/10.1007/978-3-030-88421-5_1

Science (SJD/JSD) program is often structured as an integrated doctoral program. We shall refer to professional doctorates and integrated doctorates in Chap. 3, albeit in a limited manner since the two awards in law are only found where the American-styled doctoral system obtains.

This book provides a critically insightful study of various doctoral programs in law, especially in the English-speaking world. In so doing, it provides a conceptual and theoretical framework for the development of effective doctoral programs in law, contending that the point of a doctorate is that it recognizes an independent contribution to the subject rather than taught coursework, however advanced.[1] The book goes on to examine the concept of a higher doctorate in law as a possible mechanism of strengthening the concept of a law doctorate in legal academia. In collecting data for this book, an area where there was a dearth of literature relates to empirical evidence pertaining to statistical and quantitative data on the number of SJD or JSD students enrolled or graduated annually across the country, compared, say, to JD students.[2] Although the American Bar Association (ABA) provides some aggregate data on its website of JD enrolments in the US annually, ABA does not often desegregate post-JD data pertaining to Master of Laws (LLM) degree enrolments and JSD or SJD degree enrolments.[3] The numbers for all post-JD enrolments are often lumped together, making it difficult to determine the statistics pertaining exclusively to JSD or SJD enrolments.[4] What is, however, clear is that the total number of post-JD enrolments does not come anywhere near half of the total number of JD enrolments,[5] signifying the area of emphasis for resource allocation in US law schools. According to a recent 2020 report by ABA,

> ABA-approved law schools are required to post their Standard 509 Information Reports on their websites as part of their ABA Required Disclosures, annually by December 15. The ABA Section of Legal Education and Admissions to the Bar website provides access to that information for all law schools, including downloadable spreadsheets of aggregate data that the law schools report. The Section is also providing spreadsheets on a school-by-school basis that report applicant data and LSAT and UGPA information for each school's 1L matriculants, changes in the 1L classes on a school-by-school basis, and other information. These data come from the annual questionnaires that ABA-approved law schools file with the Section of Legal Education and Admissions to the Bar's Managing Director's Office.[6]

The 2020 ABA report provides further:

> …197 law schools that are approved by the ABA to confer the Juris Doctor (J.D.) degree reported total JD enrollment of 114,520 for the Fall 2020 term. This is an increase of 1,638 students (1.5 percent) from 2019. An additional 21,292 students were enrolled in other than J.D. degree programs (LL.M., masters and certificate programs). This is an increase of 1,473

[1] See Phillips and Pugh (1994), p. 181.

[2] *Cf* generally Hopkins (2016).

[3] American Bar Association (Online), "2020 Standard 509 Information Report Data Overview".

[4] Ibid.

[5] Ibid.

[6] Ibid.

> (7.4 percent) from 2019. This brings the total law school enrollment for Fall 2020 to 135,812, an increase of 3,128 (2.4 percent).[7]

The 2020 ABA report posits that law schools disclosed that 38,202 students began studies in the Fall 2020 1L class (plus the preceding winter/spring/summer terms for schools with multiple starts) and that this is a decrease of 81 students (−0.21%) from the 2019 reporting cycle.[8] According to ABA, 86 schools reported smaller 1L classes for this admissions cycle and 111 schools reported an increase or no change in their new 1L classes compared to 2019.[9]

It would be interesting to find out, for example, how SJD/JSD and JD degree holders compare when it comes to placement in academia, industry and elsewhere outside the US. We are, however, mindful that given the differences in the size of some US law schools as well as in the size of their JD and post-JD degree programs, such data could vary significantly across law schools and states. In fact, some US law schools hardly offer the SJD or JSD program.[10] Similar challenges exist in various English-speaking countries outside the US for readily available statistical data on the British-styled law doctorate. And so, our study proceeds with a qualitative methodology that is supported by international and comparative perspectives to enrich objectivity and provide a critical and integrated analysis.

This book is written against the backdrop of the recently adopted Global Convention on the Recognition of Qualifications concerning Higher Education 2019. The said treaty was adopted by the 40th session of the United Nations Educational, Scientific and Cultural Organization (UNESCO) General Conference in Paris on November 25, 2019, making it the first United Nations treaty on higher education with a global scope.[11] As UNESCO posits:

> Today over 5.3 million students are pursuing their higher education abroad. This represents 2 out of every 100 students, and half of them are studying outside their home region. The rapid growth in international mobility at the university level is likely to continue. The Global Convention is designed to facilitate international academic mobility and promote the right of individuals to have their higher education qualifications evaluated through fair, transparent and non-discriminatory manners.[12]

The principal aims of this Convention, UNESCO submits, are to expand access to higher education around the world by facilitating international exchanges of students, teachers, researchers and job-seekers as well as to strengthen international cooperation in higher education and contribute to raising its quality worldwide.[13] In the quest

[7] Ibid.

[8] Ibid.

[9] Ibid.

[10] See American Bar Association (Online), "LLM and Post-JD Degrees by School".

[11] See UNESCO (Online), "2019 Global Convention on the Recognition of Qualifications concerning Higher Education: the Global Convention opens a world of opportunities and mobility for students".

[12] Ibid.

[13] See Ibid. See also European Convention on the Equivalence of Diplomas leading to Admission to Universities (1953, ETS No. 15) and its Protocol (1964, ETS No. 49); European Convention on

to meet a key aspiration of the Convention, namely, that "the international recognition of qualifications concerning higher education will facilitate interdependent learning and knowledge development", what then is a doctorate degree?

In their treatise, *Getting a Ph.D. in Law*, Morris and Murphy, make a bold attempt at defining a doctorate degree, contending that some people simply say that a Ph.D. is a book, while others say that a Ph.D. is the development and communication of a question to which one proffers an answer.[14] A more detailed definition of a doctorate, Morris and Murphy aver,[15] comes from the UK Quality Assurance Agency for Higher Education (QAA), the body responsible for auditing higher education institutions in the UK,[16] positing that:

---

the Equivalence of Periods of University Study (1956, ETS No. 21); European Convention on the Academic Recognition of University Qualifications (1959, ETS No. 32); Convention on the Recognition of Studies, Diplomas and Degrees concerning Higher Education in the States belonging to the Europe Region (1979); and the European Convention on the General Equivalence of Periods of University Study (1990, ETS No. 138). *Cf*. the Convention on the Recognition of Qualifications concerning Higher Education in the European Region developed by the Council of Europe and UNESCO and adopted by national representatives meeting in Lisbon from April 8 to April 11, 1997. Most European countries have since ratified this Council of Europe/UNESCO Convention—usually referred to as the "Lisbon Convention". As the Council of Europe observes (Council of Europe (2021) Higher Education and Research. https://www.coe.int/t/dg4/highereducation/Recognition/LRC_en.asp. Accessed 01 January 1, 2021): "Among the main points of the Council of Europe/UNESCO Convention are the following: Holders of qualifications issued in one country shall have adequate access to an assessment of these qualifications in another country; No discrimination shall be made in this respect on any ground such as the applicant's gender, race, colour, disability, language, religion, political opinion, national, ethnic or social origin; The responsibility to demonstrate that an application does not fulfil the relevant requirements lies with the body undertaking the assessment; Each country shall recognise qualifications—whether for access to higher education, for periods of study or for higher education degrees—as similar to the corresponding qualifications in its own system unless it can show that there are substantial differences between its own qualifications and the qualifications for which recognition is sought; Recognition of a higher education qualification issued in another country shall have one or more of the following consequences: *access to further higher education studies, including relevant examinations and preparations for the doctorate, on the same conditions as candidates from the country in which recognition is sought; The use of an academic title, subject to the laws and regulations of the country in which recognition is sought; In addition, recognition may facilitate access to the labour market*: All countries shall develop procedures to assess whether refugees and displaced persons fulfil the relevant requirements for access to higher education or to employment activities, even in cases in which the qualifications cannot be proven through documentary evidence; All countries shall provide information on the institutions and programmes they consider as belonging to their higher education systems; All countries shall appoint a national information centre, one important task of which is to offer advice on the recognition of foreign qualifications to students, graduates, employers, higher education institutions and other interested parties or persons; All countries shall encourage their higher education institutions to issue the Diploma Supplement to their students in order to facilitate recognition. The Diploma Supplement is an instrument developed jointly by the European Commission, the Council of Europe and UNESCO that aims to describe the qualification in an easily understandable way and relating it to the higher education system within which it was issued".

[14] Morris and Murphy (2011), p. 11.

[15] Ibid., p. 12.

[16] Ibid., pp. 11–12.

Doctorates are awarded to students who have demonstrated:

(a) the creation and interpretation of new knowledge, through original research or other advanced scholarship, of a quality to satisfy peer review, extend the forefront of the discipline, and merit publication;
(b) a systematic acquisition and understanding of a substantial body of knowledge which is at the forefront of an academic discipline or area of professional practice;
(c) the general ability to conceptualize, design and implement a project for the generation of new knowledge, applications or understanding at the forefront of the discipline, and to adjust the project design in the light of the unforeseen problems;
(d) a detailed understanding of applicable techniques for research and advanced academic inquiry.[17]

Based on this QAA definition of a doctorate, Morris and Murphy contend that a "doctorate concerns the creation of new knowledge through a rigorous process of research and reporting."[18] Recognized widely as a terminal degree, a doctorate is often the most advanced degree that an individual can get in an academic discipline. As the QAA observes,

> The doctoral degree is one of the most well-known and well-established postgraduate qualifications. The PhD (or DPhil in some universities) is the main doctoral qualification in the UK. Since the early 1990s, however, the form of the UK doctorate has diversified, leading to differently structured degrees to accommodate the needs of increasingly diverse professions employing doctoral graduates. Doctorates other than the PhD have evolved, leading to the emergence of the titles 'professional' doctorate, and 'practice-based' or 'practice-led' doctorate.[19]

In the US, a view has been expressed that a doctorate is a terminal degree, meaning that it is the highest possible degree available in an academic field.[20] Doctorates are said to be either applied or research-based and that they often attract learners who already hold a master's degree.[21]

> A doctor of philosophy degree, or PhD, emphasizes research. Students in PhD programs spend most of their time conducting research projects and studies. On the other hand, applied doctorates — like a juris doctor or doctor of pharmacy — emphasize practical applications of skills and knowledge. These degrees often also include a research component.[22]

Interestingly, a JD degree does not usually attract candidates with a masters degree, unless in exceptional cases where a foreign trained lawyer who already holds a foreign

[17] Ibid., p. 12.

[18] Ibid.

[19] UK Quality Assurance Agency for Higher Education (Online), "Characteristics Statement: Doctoral Degree".

[20] See TBS Staff (Online), "What is a doctoral degree?"

[21] See generally Ibid.

[22] See generally Ibid.

or US master of laws (LLM) degree decides to pursue a JD. Another definition of a doctorate in the US stipulates that:

> A doctorate degree is the highest level of academic degree in most fields. For research or university teaching, the degree is usually a PhD, while applied professional doctorates include the Doctor of Medicine (MD), the Doctor of Education (EdD), and the Juris Doctor (JD), among others. But, you can earn a doctorate in almost any subject area. For example, most states require licensed psychologists to hold a doctorate degree in psychology. Typically a doctorate degree takes four years to complete, post-bachelor's degree. If you already hold a master's degree, you may be able to complete a doctorate in the same subject area with only three years of additional full-time study.[23]

Having outlined the key objective of this study and provided a working definition of a doctoral degree, we now proceed to identify the main research questions.

1.2 Research Questions

A notable issue related to the main objective of the study is how legal academia outside the US and UK regards US-styled doctorates and UK-styled doctorates. Indeed, to what extent are law schools in the English-speaking world outside the UK and the US expected to follow, or align their law doctoral programs to, the American or British doctoral programs given that they follow the English common law? Or, do the varying structures of law doctoral programs in the US and the UK send a convoluted and mixed signal that offers no clear direction to law schools in other parts of the English-speaking world? What are the best practices internationally for a sound law doctoral program? These important questions because the trends and institutional or structural developments relating to law doctoral programs in the UK and the US can affect or influence the structure of similar programs in other English-speaking countries. It is important to set the context right by asking, for example, the following questions:

(a) How well is the Juris Doctor (JD) degree recognized internationally as a doctorate?
(b) How well is the Doctor of Juridical Sciences (JSD/SJD) degree recognized internationally as a doctorate?
(c) How well is a Doctor of Philosophy (Ph.D.) degree in law recognized internationally as a doctorate?
(d) What additional value can the concept of a higher doctorate bring to legal academia?
(e) To what extent does the recognition of doctoral qualifications impact on the prospects for mobility and employability of the degree-holder?

The internationalization of western legal norms is often entrenched by the fact that many legal academics in Africa and Asia as well as in the Caribbean and Pacific

[23] GetEducated (Online), "What is a doctorate degree?"

countries continue to obtain their law doctorates from the US and the UK. This feature can impact on how these academics view the suitability of certain models of law doctorates transplanted from the UK or the US to their home countries. A question could be asked, for example, to what extent does an American SJD or JSD measure up to a British Ph.D. in Law within the US or the UK as well as outside the two countries?

As we shall see in Chap. 2 of this book, the University of Yale Law School, which ranks consistently as the best law school in the US, has ended up introducing a Ph.D. in Law program designed exclusively for American trained JD-holders, pushing all foreign-trained lawyers to the JSD program.[24] Equally important is how the American JD degree compares, as a 'doctorate', to law doctorates from outside the US. Indeed, how is the American JD viewed outside the US? Is it considered as a terminal degree or the equivalent of a Ph.D. in Law or not? How has legal academia outside the US responded to claims that the American JD is a doctorate degree? Indeed, what is a real doctorate in legal academia?

1.3 A Quest for World-Class Doctoral Programs in Law

Although there is no universal definition of a world-class doctoral program, it could be argued that a doctoral program that is not respected by the people who designed it cannot qualify as a world-class doctoral program. Indeed, if the 'owners' of the program themselves are not eager to take doctoral degrees under such a program, how can outsiders or anyone else claim that those doctoral degrees are world-class awards? Put simply, a world-class doctoral program is one that is respected firstly by the people that designed the program, and, secondly, by the general academic community worldwide. Indeed, a world-class doctoral program has a universal appeal and is not reserved mainly for outsiders or some marginalized section of the community.

In general, whereas the ranking of universities often points to academic institutions that could be considered as world-class universities,[25] the ranking of law schools, by contrast, especially in the US, focusses mainly on the JD degree program and hardly factors in the JSD or SJD program.[26] Post-JD programs such as the LLM and the JSD or JSD are often treated as stepchildren of the JD family. By contrast, the British Ph.D. in Law is not treated with such suspicion by the British academics themselves. In fact, many law professors in the UK do hold a British Ph.D. in Law, signifying a high level of trust and confidence in their doctoral programs. Seldom do legal academics in the UK or other English-speaking countries go for a Ph.D. in a cognate field, as opposed to a Ph.D. in Law, notwithstanding that lawyers in

[24] See Yale Law School (Online), "Ph.D. Common Questions: How is the Ph.D. in Law degree related to the JSD degree?"

[25] See Salmi (2009), pp 15–19, see also generally, Altbach and Salmi (2011).

[26] See Public Legal (Online) 2020 Raw Data Law School Rankings.

Commonwealth countries rarely have a pre-law degree in a cognate field to enable them pursue a Ph.D. outside law.

In some instances, some US-trained lawyers have moved to Europe to get a Ph.D. in Law, say, from the University of Cambridge, the University of Oxford or such other top European law school, avoiding the US post-JD programs of JSD or SJD. What does this tell us? It means that the JSD or SJD programs in the US do not often attract the best of JD graduates. These post-JD programs are somewhat vilified by the locals and offered mainly to foreign-trained lawyers.[27] Indeed, the main vehicle on the highway to academic excellence in US legal education is the JD, while post-JD programs such as the LLM and the JSD or SJD are relegated to the dusty backstreets. It is therefore not surprising that the University of Yale Law School has now started a Ph.D. in Law program for US-trained JD graduates only, conscribing foreign-trained lawyers into the Yale JSD program instead.[28]

By contrast, in the UK, the QAA observes that:

> It is important to benchmark the UK doctorate in a global environment in order to promote mobility and to strengthen career opportunities for UK doctoral graduates. Key factors affecting the reputation of UK doctorates include having in place adequate and rigorous quality assurance mechanisms for doctoral programmes, and the ability to demonstrate consistency of standards across varied programmes.[29]

In the US, it is doubtful that JSD or SJD programs are subjected to similar standards as those applicable to the British Ph.D.[30] In contrast to the statement highlighted above from the QAA on the standards of a British Ph.D., the America Bar Association (ABA) has the following to say about American JSD or SJD programs,

> Standard 313 of the ABA Standards for Approval of Law Schools states that an ABA-approved law school may not establish a degree program other than its JD degree program unless the school is fully approved, and the additional degree program will not detract from a law school's ability to maintain a sound JD degree program. The school must obtain acquiescence prior to commencing such a program. The ABA does not formally approve any program other than the first degree in law (JD).[31]

In essence, ABA is confirming the stepchild status of the LLM and JSD or SJD programs in the American JD family. ABA makes it clear that it has no interest in post-JD programs and that it reviews them only to determine whether their offering would have an adverse impact on a law school's ability to maintain its accreditation for the JD program.[32] Furthermore, as ABA observes, the content and requirements of the LLM, JSD or SJD degree programs are created by each law school and do not

---

[27] See generally Chap. 2.

[28] See Yale Law School, "PhD Common Questions: How is the PhD in Law degree related to the JSD degree?" *op. cit.*

[29] UK Quality Assurance Agency for Higher Education, "Characteristics Statement: Doctoral Degree," *op. cit.*, p. 4.

[30] See Ibid., p. 4.

[31] America Bar Association (Online), "Post-JD and Non-JD: Overview of Other than J.D. Programs".

[32] See Ibid.

reflect any judgment by the ABA accrediting bodies regarding the quality of those programs.[33]

Without doubt, ABA has distanced itself from any endorsement of the content and requirements of post-JD qualifications, positing firmly that the "admission requirements for such programs, particularly with regard to foreign students, vary from school to school, and are not evaluated through the ABA accreditation process".[34] What this means is that as long as a US law school can maintain ABA accreditation for its JD program, the law school is free to do whatever it chooses to do with the content and requirements of its LLM, JSD or SJD programs. Now, such a loosely regulated structure of a less systematic approach to auditing post-JD qualifications is less likely to produce world-class doctoral programs in law. In addition, only a few US law schools offer JSD or SJD programs. Even for those that offer such programs, fewer resources are devoted to these programs than the resources committed to JD programs.

Let us now turn to provide a roadmap of subsequent chapters in this book.

1.4 An Outline of Subsequent Chapters

Chapter 2 examines the concept of a doctoral degree in law in the US, with analogies drawn from parallel developments in Australia, Canada, Singapore and other pertinent common law jurisdictions with a similar model of the American-styled JSD or SJD program. It also looks at other countries that have adopted the US-styled JD and JSD or SJD degree programs. Chapter 2 then makes policy recommendations to improve the international standing of the American doctoral degree programs in law.

Chapter 3 examines the concept of the British-styled law doctorate as it obtains in the UK, the Commonwealth and other pertinent jurisdictions, maintaining that the point of a doctorate is that it recognizes an independent contribution to the subject rather than taught coursework, however advanced. Chapter 3 posits that Commonwealth countries have a better structured and more systematic approach to the concept of a law doctorate than the US, notwithstanding that countries such as Canada and Australia have a hybrid system of the American and British models of law doctorates.

Chapter 4 introduces the concept of a higher doctorate as a qualification that stands *substantially* higher than a Ph.D. at many leading universities in the Commonwealth, except for Canadian universities. Also, Chap. 4 distinguishes higher doctorates from a Ph.D. and postdoctoral fellowship, contending that the concept of a higher doctorate is a more objective benchmark for making faculty appointments to full professorship than the not-so-clear criteria at some law schools.

Chapter 5 provides an analytically critical and integrated conclusion. It brings together the main arguments in the preceding chapters and reflects on the differences in the structure and standing of the JSD or SJD degree programs and the Ph.D. in law

---

33 See Ibid.

34 See Ibid.

program. Chapter 5 also offers perspectives on the value of a higher doctorate, as a rare qualification that stands authoritatively at the apex and pinnacle of the echelon of all doctorates.

References

Altbach PG, Salmi J (eds) (2011) The road to academic excellence: the making of world-class research universities. The World Bank, Washington DC

American Bar Association, LLM and Post-JD degrees by school. https://www.americanbar.org/groups/legal_education/resources/llm-degrees_post_j_d_non_j_d/programs_by_school/. Accessed 03 June 2021

America Bar Association, Post-JD and Non-JD: overview of other than J.D. programs. https://www.americanbar.org/groups/legal_education/resources/llm-degrees_post_j_d_non_j_d/. Accessed 02 March 2021

American Bar Association, 2020 Standard 509 information report data overview. https://www.americanbar.org/content/dam/aba/administrative/legal_education_and_admissions_to_the_bar/statistics/2020-509-enrollment-summary-report-final.pdf. Accessed 03 June 2021

GetEducated (Online), What is a doctorate degree? https://www.geteducated.com/career-center/detail/what-is-a-doctorate-degree/. Accessed 03 Mar 2021

Hopkins BR (2016) SJD: What's the point of three (law degrees)? The adventures of an older lawyer who returned to law school for the third degree. WaveCloud Corporation, Colorado

Morris C, Murphy C (2011) Getting a Ph.D. in Law. Hart Publishing, Oxford and Portland

Phillips EM, Pugh DS (1994) How to get a Ph.D. Open University Press, Buckingham

Public Legal (Online), 2020 raw data law school rankings. https://www.ilrg.com/rankings/law/. Accessed 05 Feb 2021

Salmi J (2009) The challenges of establishing world-class universities. The World Bank, Washington DC

TBS Staff, What is a doctoral degree? https://thebestschools.org/degrees/what-is-a-doctorate-degree/. Accessed 02 Mar 2021

UK Quality Assurance Agency for Higher Education, Characteristics statement: doctoral degree. https://www.qaa.ac.uk/docs/qaa/quality-code/doctoral-degree-characteristics-statement-2020.pdf?sfvrsn=a3c5ca81_14. Accessed 01 Mar 2021

UNESCO, 2019 Global convention on the recognition of qualifications concerning higher education: the global convention opens a world of opportunities and mobility for students. https://en.unesco.org/themes/higher-education/recognition-qualifications/global-convention. Accessed 01 Mar 2021

Yale Law School, Ph.D. common questions: how is the Ph.D. in law degree related to the JSD degree? https://law.yale.edu/studying-law-yale/degree-programs/graduate-programs/phd-program/phd-common-questions#:~:text=Both%20are%20doctoral%20degrees%2C%20which,The%20more%20structured%20Ph.&text=Unlike%20the%20Ph.,School%2C%20not%20the%20Graduate%20School. Accessed 02 Mar 2021

Chapter 2
The Concept of the American-Styled Law Doctorate as It Obtains in the US, Canada, Australia, Singapore and Other Pertinent Jurisdictions

Abstract This chapter examines the concept of a doctoral degree in law in the US, with analogies drawn from parallel developments in Australia, Canada, Singapore and other pertinent common law jurisdictions with a similar model of the American-styled JSD or SJD program. It also looks at other countries that have adopted the US-styled JD and JSD or SJD degree programs, arguing that while most Commonwealth countries have a common approach to the concept and structure of a doctoral degree in law, the practice in the US is somewhat different. This chapter then makes policy recommendations to improve the international standing of the American doctoral degree programs in law.

Keywords Australia · Canada · Singapore · United States (US) · United Kingdom (UK) · Commonwealth · Common law · Doctor of Juridical Sciences (SJD/JSD) · Recognition of qualifications · Juris Doctor (JD) · Master of Laws (LLM) · Doctor of Philosophy in Law (Ph.D. in Law) · Most advanced law degree · American Bar Association (ABA) · Master of Philosophy in Law (MPhil in Law) · Master of Letters (MLitt) · Combined or dual JD and Ph.D. programs · Bachelor of Laws (LLB) · Doctor of Medicine (MD) · Doctor of Comparative Law · Visiting Assistant Professorships (VAP) · Judicial clerkships

2.1 Introduction

Chapter 1 provided an introduction of the study, setting out the objectives and key research questions. Also, Chap. 1 laid out the roadmap of subsequent chapters in the book. This chapter now turns to examine the concept of a doctoral degree in law in the United States of America (US), with analogies drawn from parallel developments in Australia, Canada, Singapore and other pertinent common law jurisdictions with a similar model of the American-styled JSD or SJD program. An argument is made that while most Commonwealth countries generally have a common approach to the concept and structure of a doctoral degree in law,[1] the practice in the US and the other countries mentioned above is somewhat different.[2]

---

[1] As can be seen from Ph.D. in Law programs at most established universities in the Commonwealth.

[2] See generally Manley (2019).

K. K. Mwenda, *Doctoral Degree Programs in Law*,
SpringerBriefs in Law, https://doi.org/10.1007/978-3-030-88421-5_2

Examining research training systems in Denmark, Finland, Norway and Sweden, with emphasis on the structure, organization, time span of the degree, completion rates, labor market and internationalization of postgraduate education, Kyvik and Tvede argue that even though the various national research training systems in the Nordic countries seem to be becoming more similar, there are still differences in their organizational models.[3] According to the authors, the model of the US 'graduate school' has been the inspiration and basis for many European initiatives to improve doctoral degree education.[4] Kyvik and Tvede posit that in all these countries such schools have been introduced, but often in a modified form and to a limited extent.[5] The authors conclude that the trend is towards a common international Ph.D. where the content, breadth, length and quality are equivalent.[6] Admittedly, the view presented by Kyvik and Tvede focusses on attributes of the American Ph.D. program in cognate fields outside law, not the Doctor of Juridical Science (SJD or JSD) degree programs.

In the US, the Juris Doctor (JD) degree, though considered by many US-trained lawyers as a terminal degree,[7] but not viewed as such by lawyers outside the US,[8] is recognized as the more relevant degree than, say, the Master of Laws (LLM) and the SJD or JSD, for purposes of bar admission and law practice.[9] Also, the JD is seen as the ideal qualification for purposes of pursuing an academic career in the US.[10] By contrast, outside the US, the SJD or JSD, not the JD, is the degree considered by

[3] See Kyvik and Tvede (1998), pp. 9–25.

[4] See Ibid., pp. 9–25.

[5] See Ibid., pp. 9–25.

[6] See Ibid., pp. 9–25.

[7] See S. Bogle (2017), "What is a terminal degree?", where the author states that: "Terminal degrees are somewhat more complicated when it comes to professional degrees. Earning a professional degree means a person has completed their academic studies in preparation to enter a professional field… More often the terminal degree is a doctorate. Common examples of such professional degrees are the Doctor of Medicine (MD) for physicians and the Juris Doctor (JD) for lawyers. The MD and JD are currently and widely considered terminal degrees in the US, even though other post-doctoral degrees in these fields exist. For example, the Doctor of Juridical Science (JSD) is a research doctorate in law".

A rather unusual description of the SJD program by a US Law School is that found on the website of the University of Kansas School of Law, describing the SJD as a terminal degree. The University of Kansas (2021), "Degrees for International Students: Doctor of Juridical Sciences (SJD)" notes that: "The University of Kansas School of Law is one of the few law schools in the United States to offer a Doctor of Juridical Science (SJD), the terminal degree in law".

[8] See Manley (2019), pp. 392–394.

[9] The American Bar Association (Online), "Overview of Post-JD and Non-JD Programs: Overview of Other than J.D. Programs" posits that: "Standard 313 of the ABA Standards for Approval of Law Schools states that an ABA-approved law school may not establish a degree program other than its J.D. degree program unless the school is fully approved, and the additional degree program will not detract from a law school's ability to maintain a sound J.D. degree program. The school must obtain acquiescence prior to commencing such a program. The ABA does not formally approve any program other than the first degree in law (JD)".

[10] See Leiter B (2017), "Paths to Law Teaching: Information and Advice for Persons Interested in Teaching Law".

many as a terminal degree and the nearest equivalent to a Ph.D. in Law.[11] Even in some parts of the US, the SJD or JSD, not the JD, is seen as the closest equivalent to a Ph.D. in Law.[12] Stanford University Law School, for example, describes its JSD program as "the Law School's most advanced law degree, and is considered a doctorate equivalent to a Ph.D.."[13] Similarly, the National Association for Law Placement in Washington DC describes American SJD or JSD degree programs, not JD programs, as the terminal degree programs, stating explicitly that the SJD or JSD is the 'most advanced (or terminal) law degree that would follow the earning of the LLM and JD degrees.'[14] The JD is then described as the "degree awarded after three years of prescribed study in a US law school" and that "Canadian law schools award JD or LLB (Bachelor of Laws) degrees."[15] The National Association for Law Placement describes the LLB as the "equivalent to a JD degree"[16] and that "the LLB was the law degree conferred in the US prior to establishment of the JD."[17] Let us take a more reasoned look at the concept of a law doctorate in the US.

2.2 The Concept of a Law Doctorate in the US

While many JD degree programs in the US enjoy accreditation from the America Bar Association (ABA),[18] there is no national or regional framework for the regulation of post-JD degree programs such as LLMs, JSDs or SJDs. This regulatory shortcoming, as we shall see below, explains, in part, some of the varying standards of post-JD qualifications. It is not even clear if, say, a private law school whose JD is not accredited by ABA is at liberty to offer any type of LLM, JSD or SJD degree program. Indeed, how different would such an LLM, JSD or SJD qualification be from one obtained from a law school with an ABA accredited JD program? Increasingly, a number of LLM degree programs in the US are being offered Online or as executive programs.[19] What does that tell us?

---

[11] See below. Also, as the University of Oxford (2011), "What is a DPhil?", observes: "Both 'Ph.D.' and 'DPhil' are abbreviations for 'Doctor of Philosophy', which is an advanced research qualification usually involving independent research to write an original thesis. It usually takes three to four years of full-time study or six to eight years of part-time study to complete".

Many universities in the UK and other Commonwealth countries use the acronym, 'PhD', though universities such as the University of Oxford and the University of Sussex use the acronym, 'DPhil'.

[12] See below.

[13] See Stanford University Law School (2019), "Doctor of Science of Law (JSD)".

[14] National Association for Law Placement (Online), "Working Glossary".

[15] See Ibid.

[16] See Ibid.

[17] See Ibid.

[18] See below.

[19] See for example the Northeastern University School of Law Online LLM degree program, the University of Southern California Online LLM degree program, the Georgetown University Law Center Online LLM degree program, the Georgetown University Law Center Executive LLM degree

Until recently, the two well-known law degrees in the US whose appellation carries the term, 'Doctor', are the JD and JSD or SJD.[20] Nomenclature can be misleading at times in the US.[21] Robinson observes that:

> In the United States, the most advanced degrees offered by law schools are, counter-intuitively, predominantly granted to foreigners. The LLM, or master in laws, has become a staple for law graduates from other countries hoping to further their careers back home, find a job in the US, or merely spend a year enjoying a fun experience abroad. The JSD or SJD, or doctorate of science and law, is generally targeted at foreigners wishing to teach, either back in their own country or hoping to find a job on the US academic market. Meanwhile, most US law students, including those interested in a teaching career, never even consider one of these advanced degrees, at least until the recent creation of Yale's PhD in law. How did this seemingly paradoxical situation come to be, where the most advanced law degrees are largely ignored by US students, but embraced by foreigners?[22]

In 2012, amid national scrutiny, Yale University Law School launched the first ever Ph.D. in Law degree program in the US.[23] Three students from the inaugural class of Yale Law School's Ph.D. in Law program—the first of its kind in the nation—graduated in 2016, signaling much promise for a program that faced controversy at its outset.[24] Yale Law School stipulates that the Ph.D. in Law program is designed to prepare JD graduates for careers as legal scholars and teachers through a doctoral program aimed at the production of a substantial body of academic research and writing under the close supervision of a three-member faculty dissertation committee.[25]

Yale Law School contends that, in addition to offering an opportunity to study and contribute to the evolution of law as an academic field of study, the Yale Ph.D. in Law program provides an excellent pathway to a career in legal scholarship and law teaching.[26] The Ph.D. in Law program is said to offer more value than a fellowship

---

program in Securities and Financial Regulation, the University of Arizona Online LLM degree program, the University of Dayton Law School Online LLM degree program, the Boston University Law School Online LLM degree program in tax law, the University of Pepperdine Law School Online LLM degree program in dispute resolution, the University of Delaware Online LLM degree programs, the University of Fordham Law School Online LLM degree program, the Columbia University Law School Executive LLM degree program, the Northwestern University Executive LLM degree program, the New York University Law School Executive LLM degree program in tax law, and many others.

[20] See below for the Ph.D. in Law degree programs at Yale University Law School and the University of Washington in Seattle. Also, see the Doctor of Comparative Law (D.Comp.L) degree program at the University of Chicago Law School.

[21] For example, a handyman or technician at a block of apartments is sometimes referred to as an 'engineer' while a carpet cleaner might advertise his services by referring to himself as a 'carpet doctor'. Even the guy fixing bicycles at the street-corner might describe himself as a 'bike doctor'.

[22] See Robinson N (2015), "The history of the advanced degree in law in the United States." See also generally, Hupper (2015).

[23] See Staff Reporter (2016), "First Law PhDs Set to Graduate".

[24] See generally Ibid.

[25] See Yale Law School (Online), "The Ph.D. in Law Program".

[26] See Yale Law School (Online), "Why a Ph.D. in Law?".

or a visiting assistant professorship (VAP), especially that the Ph.D. program is a three-year course of study beyond the JD and provides a more structured program—including coursework, qualifying exams, and close faculty supervision—than do most fellowships or VAPs.[27]

Prior to 2012, Yale University Law School, like many other top US Law Schools, did not have a Ph.D. in Law program. Instead, the JSD or SJD degree program was the main research degree in law, although JSD or SJD candidates were also expected to complete some coursework and qualifying exams in the initial stages of the program as well as to benefit later from close faculty supervision of their dissertation. After introducing the Ph.D. in Law degree program, Yale Law School retained the JSD degree program, arguing that both degrees are doctorates, which are the highest academic degrees in law awarded by Yale University, though the programs have different structures and are designed for different purposes.[28] The more structured Ph.D. program, according to Yale Law School, is designed specifically for students whose first degree in law is a JD from a US law school, and the Ph.D. is formally awarded by Yale University's Graduate School of Arts and Sciences.[29] By contrast, the JSD degree is designed principally for students who received their first degree in law from a non-US institution and subsequently received their LLM at Yale Law School.[30] Unlike the Ph.D., the JSD is awarded by Yale Law School, not the Graduate School.[31]

In a manner similar to the way Yale Law School describes its Ph.D. in Law program, Cornell Law School attempts to bolster the image of its JSD program by stating that,

> …Cornell Law's JSD is conferred by Cornell University, not the Law School, and is comparable to a PhD. This makes the degree more rigorous as the JSD program is run in accordance with Cornell's Graduate School policies.[32]

But, is the standard of JSD program at Cornell University at par with that of the Ph.D. in Law program at Yale University simply because both doctoral degrees are awarded by the Graduate School, not the Law School, of the respective universities? Or, is Cornell Law School's JSD program just a refashioned JSD or SJD program found at many other US Law Schools? Unlike Yale Law School which limits admission to its Ph.D. in Law program to JD graduates of US Law Schools,[33] the JSD program at Cornell Law School is designed for students who hold a first degree in law and an LLM degree from Cornell Law School (or, in unusual circumstances, the equivalent of that LLM) who want to pursue an academic career.[34] In essence, what

[27] See Ibid.

[28] Yale Law School (Online), "Ph.D. Common Questions: How is the Ph.D. in Law degree related to the J.S.D. degree?"

[29] See Ibid.

[30] See Ibid.

[31] See Ibid.

[32] Cornell Law School (Online), "JSD Admissions".

[33] See above.

[34] See Cornell Law School, "JSD Admissions", *op. cit.*

this means is that while Cornell Law School suggests that its JSD program, like Yale Law School's Ph.D. in Law program, is run in accordance with the Graduate School policies, not the Law School policies, the admission requirements to Cornell's JSD program are, unlike those applicable to Yale's Ph.D. in Law program, not limited to JD graduates of US Law Schools. Rather, foreign trained lawyers with an LLB and/or LLM from a foreign law school can be admitted to Cornell Law School's JSD program after completing an LLM degree program at Cornell.[35]

Examining the issue of perception associated with JSD or SJD programs, Robinson observes that:

> Today, despite more attention to the JSD/SJD programs at many top law schools, clear tensions exist in how schools view their American-dominated JD programs and their foreign dominated graduate programs. Both Hupper and the commentators on her piece point to Yale's recent development of a PhD in law as evidence of this unresolved strain. Hupper notes that when Yale created its new PhD program that it made explicit the degree was only for the further training of students who already have a US law degree. This, of course, is ironic as this is precisely what Yale's JSD program had been designed to do, and did with considerable success in the first half of the 20th century.[36]

Robinson continues:

> Carole Silver in her commentary argues that the PhD in law represents an attempt by Yale to reassert its centrality in the US academic hiring market, where Yale Law School now faces increasing competition to its prestige and clout from PhD programs in other disciplines. Paulo Barrozzo in his commentary though expresses concern that Yale's PhD program will relegate the JSD to a second-tier degree. Already the JSD/SJD has had to battle perceptions within the US that because it is dominated by foreigners that it is not as prestigious. The development of a PhD in law dominated by US students, but largely excluding foreigners, may only cement this perception.[37]

Be that as it may, both the JSD and Ph.D. in Law programs at Yale Law School are primarily research doctorates, though the Yale JSD, like the Cornell JSD as well as the JSD or SJD degree programs at other US Law Schools, are designed mainly for foreigners.[38] Indeed, the Yale JSD admits mainly top foreign students graduating from the Yale LLM while the Yale Ph.D. in Law is designed exclusively for top JD graduates from a US law school.[39] But one could ask: why is it that the JSD and SJD programs are offered primarily to foreigners, not Americans? The Case Western Reserve University School of Law, for example, states that "the SJD is designed to give you an opportunity to complete the highest research degree in law within a specialized field of study of your choice"[40] and that "the program will prepare you to

---

[35] See Ibid.

[36] See generally Robinson N (2015), "The history of the advanced degree in law in the United States.

[37] See Ibid. See also Hopkins (2016), pp. 3–12.

[38] See above.

[39] See above.

[40] See Case Western Reserve University School of Law (2021), "SJD Programs—Doctor of Juridical Sciences (SJD).

return to your home country to work in academia or law reform for your government at the highest level."[41] Similarly, Georgetown University Law Center posits that the "Doctor of Juridical Science (SJD) is the highest degree offered by Georgetown"[42] and that "Our students come here from all over the world; what they have in common is a desire to teach and write when they return home."[43] Even more interesting is the statement by the University of Pittsburg School of Law, stipulating that its "SJD program is only open to exceptionally well-qualified candidates who both (a) earned their first law degree *outside* of the United States and (b) have successfully completed an LLM degree at an ABA accredited law school in the US."[44] Closely related to the foregoing, the Center on the Legal Profession at Harvard Law School submits that:

> The JSD and SJD started in the late 1800's at top US law schools like Harvard, Yale, and Columbia to train US lawyers for the domestic teaching market. The rise of these degrees corresponded with that of full-time law teachers and the view of law as a standalone science. Students who were interested in a career in teaching would pursue a JSD or SJD at elite law schools, which frequently conferred a Master in Law (LLM) as an interim degree. By World War II, 20 to 25 percent of professors at top US law schools held a JSD or SJD, as did many professors at other law schools around the country.[45]

According to Harvard Law School's Center on the Legal Profession,

> After World War II, however, the degree went out of favor for those interested in the US law teaching market. Within law schools, many LLB students (the precursor to the JD) began taking many of the same classes as JSD's or SJD's. Moreover, legal practice, particularly clerkship experience, became more valued by law school hiring committees. At the same time, the realist shift in the legal academy meant that perspectives from other fields, such as economics and political science, became more prized, heightening the advantage of a PhD from another discipline for those interested in graduate study before pursuing law teaching… By the 1970s two-thirds of SJD and JSD graduates were not US citizens. Today almost none are. US students became less interested in those degrees. JSD, SJD, and LLM programs are now one of the primary ways through which US law schools extend their global reach, with graduates returning to their home countries to teach and practice after being exposed to American legal pedagogy and understandings of law. The metamorphosis of these advanced degrees from a tool for training US law teachers to a tool for training foreign lawyers was organic. Today, and in many ways as a response to the devaluation of the SJD and JSD in the US legal academy, Yale Law School recently began a PhD in law to train US students for the US teaching market."[46]

---

[41] See Ibid.

[42] See Georgetown University Law Center (Online), "SJD degree".

[43] See Ibid.

[44] See University of Pittsburgh School of Law (Online), "Doctor of Juridical Science (SJD) Program".

[45] See Center on the Legal Profession, Harvard Law School (2015), "American Degree Goes Global: The transformation of the Doctorate of Science and Law".

[46] See Ibid.

Although many US law schools that offer the JSD or SJD degree programs describe these degrees as the 'most advanced law degree' designed primarily for those interested in becoming scholars and teachers of law,[47] the assumption is that most graduates of these programs will become scholars and teachers of law elsewhere, not in the US.[48] Mui observes that:

> What are the reasons to get a JSD (also called an SJD) degree? St. John's University School of Law assistant professor Marc DeGirolami, who just finished a JSD at Columbia Law School, is curious to see if the degree, which is most often pursued by foreign law graduates, will eventually catch on among US law graduates. Candidates for a Scientiae Juridicae Doctor degree not only already have their JDs, but also their LLMs, DeGirolami writes.[49]

According to Mui, for US trained lawyers who choose to pursue the SJD or JSD degree, it is designed for those interested in academic legal careers and might be of particular value to those who "at least in some measure [want] to burnish a CV with a JD from a non-elite law school (say, a school outside the top 5 or 7)."[50] Mui notes further that, if a U.S. law grad is "using the JSD as a way to polish up what will be perceived as some ugly soiling on your CV" he or she should only pursue a JSD at one of the nation's top law schools.[51] Mui posits that, at the same time, that JSDs are not universally respected by academic employers and that some academic employers 'don't know what to make' of the degree.[52] Mui recalls that back in 2008, a reader of *Brian Leiter's Law School Reports* asked the University of Chicago law professor about the relative value of a JSD, and that Prof Leiter responded as follows:

> The strong interdisciplinary turn of law schools over the past 30 years means that the credential of real value to an American lawyer is a PhD in a cognate discipline, not a 'PhD' in law.[53]

Further, the 'devaluation' of the JSD and SJD degrees in the US legal academy has been made worse by the explicit pronouncement by the American Bar Association

---

[47] See for example, Stanford University Law School (2020), "The Doctor of the Science of Law (JSD) Degree." See also Harvard Law School (2020), "SJD Program".

[48] On its website, Georgetown University Law School, for example, postulates that: "The Doctor of Juridical Science (SJD) is the highest degree offered by Georgetown. Our students come here from all over the world; what they have in common is a desire to teach and write when they return home".

(See Georgetown University Law School (2021) SJD Degree. https://www.law.georgetown.edu/academics/graduate-programs/degrees/s-j-d-degree/. Accessed 02 June 2021).

Also, the Case Western University School of Law, on its website, maintains a similar view, contending that: "The SJD…will prepare you to return to your home country to work in academia or law reform for your government at the highest level".

(See Case Western University School of Law (2021) SJD Programs. https://case.edu/law/academics/sjd-programs. Accessed 02 June 2021).

[49] Mui S (2010), "Should Aspiring Law Profs Go for a JSD Degree?"

[50] See Ibid.

[51] See Ibid.

[52] See Ibid.

[53] See Ibid. Here, reference to 'Ph.D. in Law' relates to the JSD or SJD degrees in the US, not the PhD in Law offered elsewhere outside the US.

(ABA) that "ABA does not formally approve any program other than the first degree in law (JD)."[54] ABA makes it clear that ABA accreditation covers only the JD degree and "does not extend to any program supporting any other degree granted by the law school" and that "the content and requirements of those degrees…are created by the law school itself."[55] Thus, it would appear that the rubric that appears on many US law school websites, describing the JSD or SJD as the 'most advanced law degree', is nothing but a marketing ploy to attract unsuspecting foreigners to pursue graduate legal studies in the US. Indeed, as ABA notes,[56] the content and requirements of these degrees, that is, the LLM, the JSD or the SJD, are created by each concerned law school itself. As a result, the standards and structure of the JSD or SJD degree programs vary from one US Law School to another.[57] For example, some top US law schools such as Harvard,[58] Columbia,[59] Pennsylvania,[60] and Georgetown[61] permit the option of a doctoral candidate submitting three law review articles for the award of the JSD or SJD degree. It is not clear if other US law schools have provision for such a practice, although the Yale Ph.D. in Law program offer the option.[62] This practice of submitting three law review articles in lieu of a traditional monograph-style doctoral dissertation is akin to the British Ph.D. by Published Work which is also found at most established law schools in other Commonwealth countries.[63]

Furthermore, because the structure and standards of each JSD, SJD and Ph.D. in Law program are set independently by each concerned US law school, the word limit of some SJD and JSD dissertations seems to vary across the board. It is even more worrying that the US does not have the equivalent of a two year British research masters degree in law such as the Master of Philosophy (MPhil in Law) or the Master of Letters (MLitt in Law) for dissertations that are more extensive than an LLM thesis, but not as substantial as a PhD in Law dissertation.[64] The development of such two year research degree programs can help the concerned US law school ensure that their JSD and SJD dissertations are above the standard of the MPhil in Law and MLitt in Law dissertations. Compared to the US, the British system of legal education and

---

[54] See the American Bar Association (ABA), "Overview of Post-JD and Non-JD Programs: Overview of Other than J.D. Programs," *op. cit.*

[55] See Ibid.

[56] See above.

[57] For example, some US law schools permit the option of submitting three law review articles for the award of the JSD or SJD degree. This practice is akin to the PhD by Published Work that exists at most established universities in the Commonwealth. That said, other US Law Schools insist on the submission of a book-length dissertation. Also, the word limit of some SJD and JSD dissertations seems to vary across the board.

[58] See Harvard University Law School (2021), "Academics: SJD Candidates".

[59] See Columbia University Law School (Online) "JSD Admissions.".

[60] See University of Pennsylvania Carey Law School (Online), "SJD Requirements".

[61] See Phelan A.J. (2019), "Three articles written by Alexandra J. Phelan in partial satisfaction of the requirements for the S.J.D. degree".

[62] See Yale University Law School, (Online) "PhD Program Details".

[63] See generally Smith (2015).

[64] As evidenced by a survey conducted by this author over the last five years (2015–2020).

that found in other Commonwealth countries appears to have a more systematic approach to the concept and structure of a law doctorate. The following three figures hereunder help to explain the common typologies and routes to a doctoral degree for lawyers in the US (Fig. 2.1).

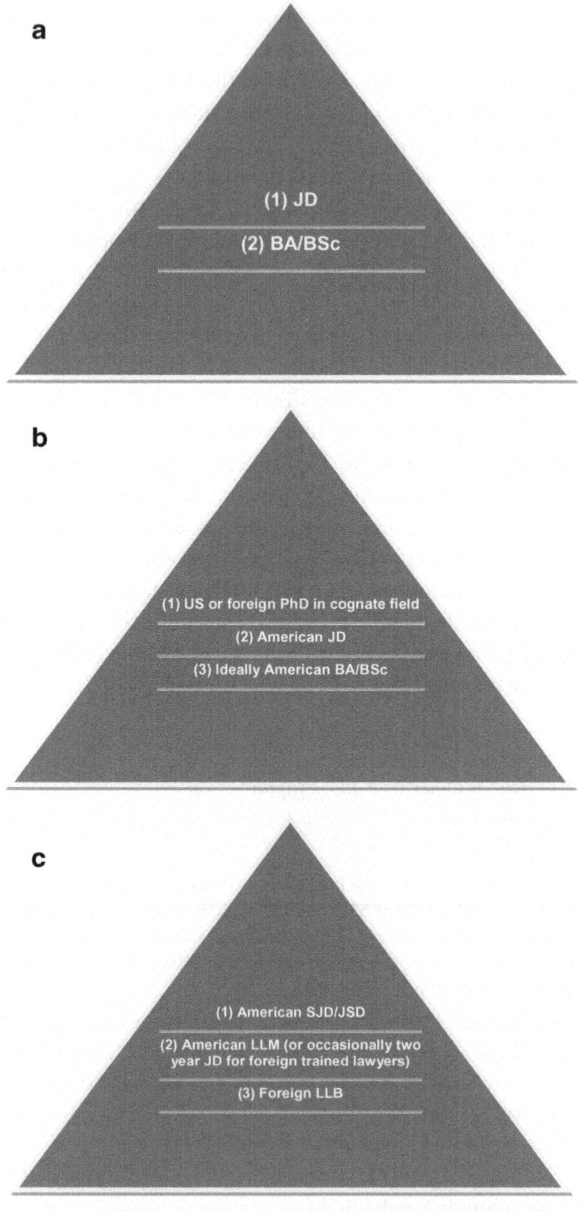

Fig. 2.1 **a** Traditional model 'A' for the US legal education system, **b** model 'B' for the US legal education system, **c** model 'C' for foreign trained lawyers under the US legal education system

It is also not uncommon to find an American JD degree holder pursuing a Ph.D. in Law program abroad, say, at a British university. The British Ph.D. in Law is considered by many as a more valuable doctoral qualification than its counterpart, the American JSD or SJD.[65] Equally, it is not unusual to find a foreign trained lawyer who holds an American LLM degree pursuing a British Ph.D. in Law.[66] Again, the same reason applies here for shunning the American JSD or SJD. Be that as it may, in some exceptional cases, it is not unusual to find an American JD degree holder pursuing an American LLM, JSD or SJD degree program.[67] These exceptional cases are common where[68]:

(a) A JD is offered as a joint four-year program with an LLM, as opposed to the traditional three-year JD;
(b) The JD was obtained from a lowly ranked US law school or the JD degree-holder graduated with poor grades, but now wants to 'cleanse' his résumé with an LLM degree from a top-tier Ivy League School; or,
(c) The LLM or JSD/SJD is in a highly specialized field such as taxation.

Following below is an examination of some combined or dual JD-PhD programs as well as other types of law-related doctoral programs in the US.

2.2.1 *Combined or Dual JD and Ph.D. Programs and Other Variants of Doctoral Programs*

Closely related to the Ph.D. in Law program at Yale University Law School, the University of Washington School of Law in Seattle offers a Ph.D. in Law program and provides that its program has been existence since 1966.[69] It is, however, not clear if the University of Washington PhD in Law program has been known as a 'Ph.D. in Law' from inception or it was renamed recently from JSD or SJD to Ph.D. in Law. Unlike the Yale Ph.D. in Law degree program, the University of Washington Ph.D. in Law degree program is not limited to US-trained lawyers with a JD and is offered within the Law School.

Other variants of US doctoral degree programs in law-related fields exist and are structured as a JD/Ph.D. in a cognate field, JD/MD (Doctor of Medicine) or Ph.D. in Law and a cognate field.[70] To illustrate, Vanderbilt University Law School has a dual-degree program that offers a law degree (JD) and a Ph.D. concurrently in a fully-integrated curriculum combining economic theory and methodology with the

[65] As evidenced from several discussions, stretching over a period from 1995 to the present, with colleagues who hold combinations of these degrees.

[66] See Ibid.

[67] See Ibid.

[68] See Ibid.

[69] See University of Washington School of Law (Online), "Ph.D. in Law".

[70] See below.

study of law.[71] This dual-degree program allows students to complete both degrees in just six years.[72] Closely related to this, George Mason University[73] and American University[74] offer Ph.D. programs in 'Criminology, Law and Society' and 'Justice, Law and Criminology', respectively, while the University of California at Berkeley offers a Ph.D. program in Jurisprudence and Social Policy (JSP)[75] as well as a separate JSD program.[76] American University also has a separate SJD program.[77] Then, the Thomas R. Kline School of Law at Drexel University and the Department of Psychology in Drexel's College of Arts and Sciences offer a joint and integrated JD/Ph.D. Program in Law and Psychology.[78] Similarly, the University of Illinois at Urbana-Champaign offers a joint JD and Ph.D. in International Relations.[79] To receive this joint JD-Ph.D., students must satisfy all requirements for the Ph.D. in Political Science, including "major and minor field course requirements, scope and methods sequence, tools, qualifying examinations, dissertation design seminar, and dissertation project".[80] As the University of Illinois at Urbana-Champaign explains:

> Joint degree students would be allowed to count 16 hours of law credit toward their PhD. Joint degree students would elect International Relations as their major area, and up to 8 hours of law school course credit would count toward this area. In addition, joint degree students will be permitted to select 'Law' as their minor field, using 8 hours of law credit to satisfy minimum course requirements, provided such credit is from course outside the international law subfield (e.g., American constitutional law); this presents a new option for international relations students who otherwise would have to select American politics, comparative politics, or political theory as a minor field. This program allows an exception to the simultaneous conferral rule in that the JD may be conferred prior to completion of the PhD degree.[81]

Against this background, let us now turn to examine the relationship between the JSD or SJD degree programs and the JD degree programs.

---

[71] See Vanderbilt University Law School (2016), "Ph.D. program in Law and Economics".

[72] See Ibid.

[73] See George Mason University College of Humanities and the Social Sciences (Online), "Ph.D. in Criminology, Law and Society".

[74] See American University School of Public Affairs (Online), "PhD in Justice, Law and Criminology."

[75] See University of California at Berkeley Law School (Online), "Jurisprudence and Social Policy".

[76] See University of California at Berkeley Law School (2021), "Jurisprudence and Social Policy".

[77] See American University Washington College of Law (Online), "SJD Program".

[78] See Drexel University College of Arts and Sciences (Online), "JD/PhD in Law and Psychology."

[79] University of Illinois at Urbana-Champaign (2018), "Political Science, PhD & Law, JD: for the joint degrees in Juris Doctor of Law and Doctor of Philosophy in Political Science".

[80] See Ibid.

[81] See Ibid.

2.3 A Battle of Doctorates Between the SJD or JSD and the JD in the US, Canada, Australia, Singapore and Other Pertinent Jurisdictions

In contrast to the JSD and SJD degree programs, the JD degree in the US, Canada and Australia is not a research degree and is offered through taught coursework. Although the American, Canadian and Australian JD degree is typically taken as a three-year graduate degree after completing a three to four year undergraduate degree in a cognate field, the curriculum of the JD is almost identical to that of the three to four year undergraduate Bachelor of Laws (LLB) degree at many established universities in other common law jurisdictions. Indeed, both the JD and LLB are first professional law degrees.

Manley, however, puts up a spirited argument that the American JD degree is different from the LLB degree offered at universities in other common law jurisdiction, contending that:

> Unlike in the United States, law in Malaysia is studied at the undergraduate level, and nearly all of my Malaysian colleagues have PhDs in law (or are in the process of earning them). Some see the JD as a type of bachelor's degree, implying that Americans whose highest degree is the JD are not qualified to teach in a university. Indeed, when I interviewed for positions I was informed that my degrees (I have a BA, an MA and a JD) were insufficient to teach the undergraduate law students in the Bachelor of Laws (LLB) program, but that an exception would be made provided that I concurrently enroll in a PhD in law program. This surprised me because in the United States, a JD qualifies one to teach law at the postgraduate level, including for degree programs higher than the JD, such as for the Master of Laws (LLM) and Doctor of Juridical Science (SJD or JSD). At the time, I felt that equating the JD with a bachelor's degree, or even a master's, was a grave mischaracterization. After completing the research for this article, however, I have come to empathize with my Malaysian colleagues and human resources officers, because although the JD is well-known in the United States and is increasingly offered in other countries, it is a perplexing degree to value.[82]

While Manley contends that the disagreement over the value of the JD can be frustrating and, in some instances, feel discriminatory,[83] many universities outside the US recognize the JSD or SJD degree, not the JD, as the near equivalent of a Ph.D. in Law.[84] Despite the fact that some taught coursework on the American LLM and JSD or SJD degree programs is carved out of the JD curriculum, and that the American LLM and JSD or SJD degrees lack ABA accreditation, many foreign universities continue to treat the American LLM and JSD or SJD degrees as more advanced degrees than the JD degree.[85] Manley acknowledges, however, that for foreign universities considering hiring candidates with a JD, the lack of an

---

[82] Manley S (2019), p. 393.

[83] Ibid., p. 393.

[84] This is evident from the high number of JSD or SJD graduates who take up academic appointments at universities outside the USA. Foreign students intending to pursue an academic career hardly ever go for the JD degree when they come to the USA, especially that they understand the JD as a first professional law degree.

[85] See Ibid.

easily determinable equivalency can lead to confusion, delay, and extra administrative work.[86] Manley observes further that attempts have been made to centralize and streamline recognition of academic qualifications generally, but that their impact remains limited.[87]

In trying to distinguish the JD degree from the LLB degree while making a case that the JD degree qualifies one to teach at university-level, Manley posits that:

> In many countries, including the United States, complicated procedures to determine equivalency continue to be used. Research is scarce in this area, and few solutions have been proposed beyond international conventions and cooperation (which have lagged). The JD is particularly problematic, because it is not like an LLB, LLM, SJD or PhD.[88]

Unfortunately, Manley does not explain how different the JD degree is from the other degrees. He simply puts forward the above statement without an explanation. Indeed, if the JD is different from the LLB, why then do universities such as Yale University Law School and the University of Washington in Seattle have a Ph.D. in Law program? Why not just stick to the JD? It is our humble submission that the content of the JD degree, as noted above, despite the JD being a three year post-bachelors degree (or sometimes a two year post-bacheors degree program for individuals with an LLB from other common law countries who wish to practice law in the US[89]), is almost same as that of the undergraduate LLB degree program at established universities in the Commonwealth. That said, to give credit to the JD program, in contrast to the LLB, since the JD is a degree taken only after completing a bachelors degree in a cognate field (or after completing an LLB at a law school outside the US), the idea of interdisciplinary studies is quite strong in the US legal academy. As Robinson points out:

> ...arguably these same contextualizing features are also part of its great strength. US law schools at their best train legal technicians, equipped to borrow methodologies and insights from other fields to solve the challenge at hand. This leads US law faculties to make large investments in exploring the intricacies of US law and its relationship with US history, politics, and economics to find context specific solutions for legal problems facing US society.[90]

Robinson is, however, quick to acknowledge that although the methodologies of disciplines outside law tend to be relevant to US legal education, this is may not be so for legal education in other countries, notwithstanding that in fields such as international law or corporate law issues are fairly similar across jurisdictions.[91] A key challenge facing US legal education today is how to ensure that it continues to provide leadership globally for the study of law while producing scholarship

86 Manley S (2019), p. 393.

87 Ibid., p. 393.

88 Ibid., p. 393.

89 See Durrani A. (2020), "Why Foreign-Trained Lawyers Should Consider a 2-Year J.D".

90 See generally Robinson N (2015), "The history of the advanced degree in law in the United States".

91 See Ibid.

that offers solutions to US legal and policy issues of both practical and theoretical relevance.[92] Should the internationalization of legal education supersede the national agenda, or should the national interests of legal education take priority? Somewhere in-between the chasm, the US must find the right balance.

Interestingly, Australia, Canada and Singapore, three Commonwealth countries that have adopted the American JD degree model, take a different view from that espoused by Manley above.[93] The University of Sydney describes the difference between a JD and an LLB as follows:

> Both the JD and the Bachelor of Laws (LLB) lead to professional accreditation to practise law. The LLB is for those commencing law studies from high school and the JD is for those who already have a degree.[94]

This statement from the University of Sydney does not suggest that the JD is at a higher pecking order or stands higher on the academic echelon than the LLB. The statement simply indicates that one program admits students straight from high school whilst the other admits students who already have a degree in a cognate field. Similarly, in Singapore, the National University of Singapore (NUS) provides the following statement:

> The Juris Doctor (JD) degree is a graduate law degree that may lead to qualification for the practice of law in Singapore. At NUS, you may select from one of two JD programmes: (i) a 2-year single graduate degree programme for candidates holding a basic law degree from another jurisdiction; or (ii) a 3-year single graduate degree programme for candidates holding a non-law degree. The 3-year JD will replace the Graduate LLB (GLB) programme, and it can be completed in 2.5 years in exceptional circumstances.

Indeed, the position put forward by the National University of Singapore is consistent with that postulated by the University of Sydney in Australia.[95] The JD in both countries is not treated as superior to the LLB.[96] Even the curricula of the JD and LLB are almost identical.[97] In Canada, the University of Toronto says the following about the JD:

> In Canada, the first-level common law degree is the *Juris Doctor* or JD, which takes three years to complete. It is an undergraduate degree program, and not a graduate degree program, even though prior undergraduate education is required for entry.[98]

Until the end of apartheid, South Africa had a similarly structured first professional law degree program as that found in the US, Canada, Australia and Singapore, that is, the JD program in the said four countries.[99] South Africa, however, retained the

---

92 See Ibid.

93 See above.

94 University of Sydney Law School (Online), "What is the difference between an LLB and a JD?"

95 See above.

96 See above.

97 See above.

98 University of Toronto Faculty of Law, "Earn your law degree".

99 See generally Dzedze (2017), pp. 107–119.

title of its law degree as a 'Bachelor of Laws' or 'LLB', notwithstanding that it could only be taken after one had completed a bachelors degree in a cognate or law-related field.[100] Even the current American JD degree was known previously as an 'LLB' degree.[101] Manley, however, admits that:

> American law graduates seeking to teach abroad need to know that, at least in my experience, foreign hiring committees consider only the SJD or PhD in law as sufficient qualification to teach law, and either do not know or decline to consider that in the United States, the JD qualifies one to teach law at the university level... Although studies show that today US law schools are hiring more academics with PhDs in cognate fields (such as economics, political science, and psychology) than ever, the majority of law faculty continue to hold the JD as their highest degree. One scholar predicts that the number of US law faculty with PhDs even at the top twenty-six schools will not exceed fifty percent until 2028, and my own research shows that even at top-ranked Yale Law School, only forty-one percent (fifty of 123) of faculty members hold doctorates arguably higher than the JD (PhDs, JSDs, MDs and foreign law doctorates). This discrepancy—between how the JD is valued at home and abroad—resonates with me personally because of the difficulties I have had in explaining my US law degree to my colleagues and human resources departments in Southeast Asia.[102]

So, what is the way forward out of this conundrum regarding how the American JD is valued differently at home and abroad? Even the view that a JD is a professional doctorate like the Doctor of Medicine (MD) degree for medical doctors, given that both degrees are usually completed after seven years of university education, or that the JSD or SJD is by contrast an academic doctorate, is not free from illogical difficulties. The US legal academy itself does not treat the JSD or SJD as a valuable academic doctorate for a law teaching career in the US.[103] Similarly, the legal academy outside the US does not treat the JD as a real doctorate, professionally or academically.[104] Robinson posits that:

> As Silver notes in her commentary, top US MBA programs are much more internationalized than top US law programs. However, perhaps this is to be expected – the result of a provincialism that is at least partially inherent to the study of law, but arguably accentuated by the approach to legal studies in the United States. For example, in many countries, law students are required to take jurisprudence. If there is a globally shared cannon in the study of law it is probably the writings of Hans Kelsen, H.L.A. Hart, or Dworkin. However, this tradition of grounding law in first principles has been frequently and openly shunned in the US, where jurisprudence is not only not a required class, but, at many law schools, it is not even offered regularly.[105]

The approach in much of the US legal academy to treat LLM and JSD or SJD degree programs as the preserve of foreign-trained lawyers is seen by some commentators as helping in 'the internationalization of these advanced degrees', though this approach simply pushes the said degrees towards the margins of the US legal

[100] See Ibid., pp. 107–119.

[101] See generally Maher K (2006), "Lawyers are Doctors, Too".

[102] Manley S (2019), pp. 393–394.

[103] See above.

[104] See above.

[105] See Robinson N. (2015), "The history of the advanced degree in law in the United States".

academy.[106] Some top US law schools often insist that a foreign student who intends to pursue a JSD or SJD degree program at that US law school should first complete the school's LLM program before proceeding to the JSD or SJD program even if the student already holds an LLM from a foreign law school.[107] This requirement seems odd, especially for a foreign student who might be in possession of a decent LLM, say, from a leading British law school.[108] In Chap. 1, we posited that this book is written against the backdrop of the UNESCO Global Convention on the Recognition of Qualifications concerning Higher Education 2019 and that the said treaty speaks to the recognition of foreign academic qualifications such as an LLM degree obtained from a recognized foreign law school. Indeed, if other countries rarely question American LLM degrees, why should US law schools question LLM degrees obtained from leading universities outside the US by requiring JSD or SJD applicants with a foreign LLM to complete an American LLM, as a second masters degree, before registering for the JSD or SJD program? In the US, the curriculum of many LLM programs are carved out of the JD curriculum, meaning that LLM students often sit in the same class as JD students and take a number of courses together, whereas in the UK, for example, an LLM degree is a stand-alone graduate program above an LLB.[109] To illustrate how the curriculum of many US LLM programs are structured, let us turn to a statement appearing on the website of the University of California, Los Angeles (UCLA), School of Law, that stipulates as follows:

> Aside from the introductory course for students who do not hold a prior US law degree, there are no required courses for the LLM degree. LLM students create their own program of study from our rich selection of advanced course offerings, and take these classes alongside the law school's Juris Doctor (JD) students.[110]

---

[106] See generally Ibid.

[107] See for example the admission requirements pertaining to Yale University's JSD program at the following website: https://law.yale.edu/studying-law-yale/degree-programs/graduate-programs/jsd-program, Accessed 14 Jan 2021. See also the admission requirements pertaining to Harvard University's SJD program at the following website: https://hls.harvard.edu/dept/graduate-program/sjd-admissions/. Accessed 14 Jan 2021. However, Harvard, unlike Yale, indicates that it can accept an LLM from another top US law school.

[108] Indeed, in a 2020–21 survey conducted by this author, one student with a foreign LLB and a British LLM from the University of London had to obtain a second LLM degree from the University of Virginia School of Law before completing his SJD degree program at University Virginia. Another student with foreign LLB and LLM degrees had to obtain a second LLM from Yale University Law School before completing his JSD at Yale. A third student with a foreign LLB degree and an LLM degree from Queen's University in Canada had to obtain a second LLM from Yale University Law School before completing his JSD at Yale. A fourth student with foreign LLB and LLM degrees and a British LLM degree from the University of London had to obtain a third masters degree, the Master of the Science of Law (JSM) from Stanford University Law School, before proceeding to Stanford's JSD degree program. A fifth student with a foreign LLB and a British LLM from the University of Warwick had to obtain a second masters degree, the JSM from Stanford University Law School, before completing her JSD program at Stanford.

[109] See below.

[110] UCLA Law (2021), "LLM Degree Requirements".

The US legal academy's parochialism that ostracizes foreign legal qualifications, confining and subjecting them to the politics of the less attractive post-JD degrees, places a limit on its global relevance. In many instances, protectionist and insular-provincial tendencies militate against internationalization. In many other common law countries, a student with foreign LLB and LLM degrees from a parallel common law jurisdiction is rarely required to take a second LLM, say, by a UK law school, before registering for a PhD program in law. To resolve this conundrum, the US should not only sign and ratify the UNESCO Global Convention on the Recognition of Qualifications concerning Higher Education 2019, but should also develop a framework for the implementation of the treaty to enable, for example, US law schools to strengthen the standing of their JSD or SJD programs by recognizing parallel entry qualifications obtained in other countries. Following below are further recommendations for US law schools to strengthen the standing of their law doctorate programs.

2.4 Internationalization and Harmonization of the Structure of Law Degrees

Many decades ago, as a graduate student at Oxford, I was told by one sarcastic British scholar about a colleague of his who held a JD from a top US university that:

> Obviously, he thinks that that is a PhD, and has put the prefix of 'Dr' before his name on his office door. It's not!

As much as that statement was loaded with academic snobbery, it shed some light on how the JD is viewed generally not only outside the US, but also among many other academics who hold PhDs in various fields in the US and elsewhere, notwithstanding that the America Bar Association (ABA) has previously insisted that:

> WHEREAS, the acquisition of a Doctor of Jurisprudence degree requires from 84 to 90 semester hours of post baccalaureate study and the Doctor of Philosophy degree usually requires 60 semester hours of post baccalaureate study along with the writing of a dissertation, the two degrees shall be considered as equivalent degrees for educational employment purposes.[111]

Murphy, however, provides an insightful illustration of the conundrum associated with attempting to elevate the JD degree to the level of a PhD, explaining that:

> One of my colleagues had a JD. He argued that he should have 'Dr' before his name on his office door. The Dean disagreed, arguing that JD is not equivalent to PhD. It ended with the guy sticking a hand-written note next to the name-plate on his door, explaining that JD is equivalent to PhD. That's how legal experts resolve such problems.[112]

---

[111] The ABA website has been updated and no longer carries this statement. However, it had been published on the ABA website earlier. See for example, Mwenda K.K. (2007), pp. 21–22.

[112] See Murphy B. (2019), "Why is a JD degree equivalent to a PhD even though most law students do not publish original research?"

Outside the US, as noted above, the SJD or JSD, not the JD, is the degree considered by many as the real doctorate and terminal degree.[113] Also, parallel post-JD degrees such as the PhD in Law offered at Yale University Law School and the University of Washington in Seattle as well as the Doctor of Comparative Law at the University of Chicago are likely to be accepted as real doctorates than the JD degree. These research degrees, although having a component of some taught coursework in the initial stages, are often accepted outside the US as the Ph.D. in Law equivalent.[114] But, within the US, the JD degree, achieved by taught coursework, is seen in many legal circles as a terminal degree and, arguably, as a doctorate, although the degree-holder is not expected to use the prefix 'Dr' before his or her name.[115]

Generally, the polemics outside the US legal academy against the JD as an equivalent of a PhD have extended to the use of the 'Dr' title by the JD degree holder. Maher, however, contends that:

> Like medical school students who earn an MD and graduate school students in any number of academic disciplines who earn a PhD, most law school students also receive a doctoral degree – juris doctor, to be precise. But lawyers are much less likely to use the doctor label than physicians or PhD recipients. It might be nice to think that it's a matter of collective professional modesty, but the more likely reason is that professional conduct rules never have been clear on whether it's permissible for a lawyer to be known as doctor. (See "Tussle Over Titles," January 2006 ABA Journal, page 28.).[116]

Maher continues:

> Actually, the appellation of juris doctor is of fairly recent vintage. In 1969, as more law schools were phasing out bachelor of law (LLB) degrees in favor of the increasingly popular JD, the ABA's Committee on Professional Ethics (which later became the Standing Committee on Ethics and Professional Responsibility) issued an opinion advising lawyers not to refer to themselves as doctors. In ABA Formal Opinion 321, the committee said that its longstanding position was derived from prohibitions against 'self-laudation' set forth in the ABA Canons of Ethics.[117]

Notwithstanding that law is different from one country to another, the British legal system is more accommodating of legal education obtained from outside the UK as long as it is from a common law jurisdiction. By parity of reasoning, given that legal scholarship in the US and parallel common law jurisdictions has matured as an

---

[113] See above.

[114] See above.

[115] See below.

[116] See Maher K. (2006), "Lawyers are Doctors, Too".

[117] See Ibid., where Maher K. continues: "Less than a year later, however, the ethics committee reversed course in light of the newly adopted ABA Model Code of Professional Responsibility. Disciplinary Rule 2–102 permitted a JD or LLM (master of law) recipient to use doctor with his or her name, the committee concluded in ABA Informal Opinion 1152 (1970). Several states concurred with the ABA's new position, while others held to the prior rule. A Maine ethics opinion issued in 1979, for instance, advised lawyers that 'the title doctor is almost exclusively confined to certain health professionals and, to some extent, academics with a PhD degree and clergymen,' so a layperson who heard a lawyer referred to as doctor would assume that the lawyer was qualified in one of those professions".

academic discipline, some policy recommendations that could help to strengthen the structure of doctoral law degree programs in the US in order to give them international character beyond the national confines of the US include the following:

(1) Promoting a gradual shift from Visiting Assistant Professorships (VAP) and judicial clerkships to the Yale PhD in Law model, especially for lawyers aspiring to be academics, while retaining the existing model of some JDs pursuing a PhD in a cognate field so as to deepen interdisciplinarity[118] and provide parallel tracks that meet international standards and best practice for the legal academy;
(2) Upgrading or giving more formal recognition to the value of the JSD or SJD degrees within the US legal academy, especially that these degrees are not often treated with much 'suspicion' in other regions of the world;
(3) Giving more formal recognition to, and acceptance of, parallel qualifications from recognized and established law schools in other common law jurisdictions to encourage some degree of reciprocity of how qualifications such as the JD are viewed outside the US;
(4) Encouraging the recruitment and hire of some international faculty from parallel common law jurisdictions, as opposed to hiring mainly local JDs, with very limited or almost no presence of international faculty, to give the legal academy some international character beyond the confines of the US; and,
(5) Ensure that the supervision of PhD-level dissertations is carried out by professors who themselves hold such qualifications so that the academic standards of degrees such as JSD and SJD are not compromised.

Indeed, the practice and the teaching of law in a globalized world requires different emphasis and a different approach from that obtaining in an insular and parochially nationalistic context.[119] Writing on the value of attracting and retaining international faculty in academia, Scott argues that:

> International faculty are a key global resource – and no longer are they concentrated in a handful of developed countries. They fill important skill gaps, signal the competitiveness of higher education systems, and bring vital, and creative, transnational experiences. Yet much less is known about international faculty than international students.[120]

Indeed, the US legal academy can benefit from moving away from an insular and parochial approach of attracting and retaining almost exclusively faculty from a national pool of talent to embracing additionally some international faculty talent in order to remain competitive globally. The cross-fertilization of ideas across disciplines and jurisdictions as well as the transnational exchanges of ideas can help to bring international character to a school. After all, how else do you internationalize if you are not open to outside ideas? And what is a university if it is not about the *universal* pursuit of knowledge?

---

118 See Bosch G.S. (2020), pp. 27–48.

119 See, for example, generally Ziegler A.R. (2020), pp. 49–82.

120 Scott P (2021) *Review* – M. Yudkevich, P.G. Altbach, L.E. Rumbley (eds) (2017).

2.5 Conclusion

This chapter has examined the concept of a law doctorate in the US, with analogies drawn from parallel developments in Canada, Australia, Singapore and other pertinent common law jurisdictions that offer the American-styled JSD or SJD program. The chapter made concrete policy recommendations to improve the international standing of the American model of doctoral degree programs in law, contending that while most Commonwealth countries generally have a common approach to the concept and structure of a doctoral degree in law, the practice in the US is somewhat different. Indeed, we observed that while many JD degree programs in the US benefit from ABA accreditation, there is no national or regional framework for the regulation of such post-JD degree programs as the LLM, the JSD or SJD. This regulatory shortcoming explains, in part, some of the varying standards of post-JD qualifications.

We also submitted that the American JD degree, although considered by many US-trained lawyers as a terminal degree, is not viewed as such by lawyers outside the US. A further argument was made that although the American JD degree is recognized as a more useful degree than, say, the LLM and SJD or JSD degrees for purposes of pursuing an academic career in the US, the position is rather different outside the US. Indeed, much of the legal academy outside the US perceives the JD as the equivalent of a graduate LLB, and not a doctorate. It is the SJD or JSD, not the JD, that commands more respect in the legal academy outside the US. The SJD or JSD is the degree considered by many outside the US as a terminal degree and the nearest equivalent to a Ph.D. in Law.

References

American Bar Association, Overview of Post-JD and Non-JD programs: overview of other than J.D. programs. https://www.americanbar.org/groups/legal_education/resources/llm-degrees_post_j_d_non_j_d/. Accessed 11 Jan 2021

American University School of Public Affairs (Online) Ph.D. in justice, law and criminology. https://www.american.edu/spa/phd/phd-jlcr.cfm. Accessed 01 Jan 2021

Bogle S (2017) What is a terminal degree? https://www.snhu.edu/about-us/newsroom/2017/11/terminal-degrees#:~:text=More%20often%20the%20terminal%20degree,degrees%20in%20these%20fields%20exist. Accessed 11 Jan 2021

Bosch GS (2020) Deconstructing Myths about Interdisciplinarity: is now the time to rethink interdisciplinarity in legal education? Eur J Legal Educ 1(1):27–48

Case Western Reserve University School of Law (Online) SJD programs—Doctor of Juridical Sciences (SJD). https://case.edu/law/academics/sjd-programs. Accessed 20 Feb 2021

Center on the Legal Profession, Harvard Law School (2015) American degree goes global: the transformation of the doctorate of science and law. https://thepractice.law.harvard.edu/article/an-american-degree-goes-global/. Accessed 02 Dec 2020

Columbia University Law School (Online) JSD admissions. https://www.law.columbia.edu/admissions/graduate-admissions/jsd-admissions. Accessed 31 Dec 2020

Cornell Law School (Online) JSD admissions. https://www.lawschool.cornell.edu/admissions/graduate-legal-studies/JSD/JSD.cfm#who-is-eligible. Accessed 10 Mar 2021
Drexel University College of Arts and Sciences (Online) JD/PhD in law and psychology. https://drexel.edu/coas/academics/graduate-programs/psychology/doctorate-juris-doctorate/. Accessed 20 Jan 2021
Durrani A (2020) Why foreign-trained lawyers should consider a 2-year J.D. https://www.usnews.com/education/best-graduate-schools/top-law-schools/articles/why-foreign-trained-lawyers-should-consider-a-2-year-jd. Accessed 12 Jan 2021
Dzedze L (2017) Time on their side? A review of the four year LLB as a tool. Speculum Juris 31(Part 1):107–119
George Mason University College of Humanities and the Social Sciences (Online) Ph.D. in criminology, law and society. https://cls.gmu.edu/programs/LA-PHD-CLS. Accessed 01 Jan 2021
Georgetown University Law Center (Online) SJD degree. https://www.law.georgetown.edu/academics/graduate-programs/degrees/s-j-d-degree/. Accessed 22 Feb 2021
Harvard Law School (2020) SJD program. https://hls.harvard.edu/dept/graduate-program/sjd-program/. Accessed 11 Jan 2021
Harvard University Law School (2021) Academics: SJD candidates. https://hls.harvard.edu/dept/graduate-program/gphandbook/academics-s-j-d-candidates-2/ Accessed 01 Feb 2021
Hopkins BR (2016) SJD: What's the point of three (Law Degrees)? The adventures of an older lawyer who returned to law school for the third degree. WaveCloud Corporation, Colorado
Hupper G (2015) Educational ambivalence: the rise of a foreign-student doctorate in law. N Engl Law Rev 49:319
Kyvik S, Tvede O (1998) The doctorate in the Nordic countries. Comp Educ 34(1):9–25
Leiter B (2017) Paths to law teaching: information and advice for persons interested in teaching law. https://www.law.uchicago.edu/careerservices/pathstolawteaching. Accessed 14 Jan 2021
Maher K (2006) Lawyers are doctors, too. https://www.abajournal.com/magazine/article/lawyers_are_doctors_too. Accessed 01 Feb 2021
Manley S (2019) Degree (Un)equivalencies: the confounding case of the Juris Doctor. J Leg Educ 68(2):392–415
Mui S (2010) Should aspiring law Profs go for a JSD degree?" https://www.abajournal.com/news/article/should_aspiring_law_profs_go_for_a_jsd_degree/ Accessed 02 June 2021
Murphy B (2019) Why is a JD degree equivalent to a Ph.D. even though most law students do not publish original research? https://www.quora.com/Why-is-a-JD-degree-equivalent-to-a-PhD-event-though-most-law-students-do-not-publish-original-research. Accessed 04 Mar 2021
Mwenda KK (2007) Comparing American and British legal education systems: lessons for commonwealth African law schools. Cambria Press, New York
National Association for Law Placement (Online) Working glossary. https://www.nalp.org/workinggglossary. Accessed 02 Mar 2021
Phelan AJ (2019) Three articles written by Alexandra J. Phelan in partial satisfaction of the requirements for the S.J.D. degree. https://repository.library.georgetown.edu/handle/10822/1060431. Accessed 15 Jan 2021
Robinson N (2015) The history of the advanced degree in law in the United States. https://legalpro.jotwell.com/the-history-of-the-advanced-degree-in-law-in-the-united-states/. Accessed 10 Jun 2021
Scott P (2021) Review. In: Yudkevich M, Altbach PG, Rumbley LE (eds) (2017), International faculty in higher education: comparative perspectives on recruitment, integration, and impact. Routledge, New York and London. https://www.routledge.com/International-Faculty-in-Higher-Education-Comparative-Perspectives-on-Recruitment/Yudkevich-Altbach-Rumbley/p/book/9781138685178. Accessed 21 Feb 2021
Smith S (2015) Ph.D. by published work: a practical guide for success. Palgrave, London
Staff Reporter (2016) First law Ph.D.s set to graduate. https://yaledailynews.com/blog/2016/04/20/first-law-ph-d-s-set-to-graduate/#:~:text=Amid%20national%20scrutiny%2C%20Yale%20Law,school%20to%20offer%20a%20Ph. Accessed 15 Jan 2021

Stanford University Law School (2019) Doctor of science of law (JSD). https://law.stanford.edu/education/degrees/advanced-degree-programs/doctor-of-science-of-law-jsd/. Accessed 15 Mar 2021

Stanford University Law School (2020) The Doctor of the science of law (JSD) degree. https://law.stanford.edu/office-of-student-affairs/the-doctor-of-the-science-of-law-jsd-degree/#slsnav-overview-of-degree-requirements. Accessed 11 Jan 2021

University of California at Berkeley Law School (Online) Jurisprudence and social policy. https://grad.berkeley.edu/program/jurisprudence-social-policy/. Accessed 02 Jan 2021

University of California at Berkeley Law School (Online) Jurisprudence and social policy. https://grad.berkeley.edu/program/law/. Accessed 02 Jan 2021

UCLA Law (2021) LLM degree requirements. https://law.ucla.edu/academics/degrees/llm-program/degree-requirements. Accessed 04 Apr 2021

University of Illinois at Urbana-Champaign (2018) Political science, Ph.D. & Law, JD: for the joint degrees in Juris Doctor of Law and Doctor of Philosophy in political science. http://catalog.illinois.edu/graduate/las_law/joint-degree/political-science-phd-law-jd/. Accessed 02 Mar 2021

University of Kansas (Online) Degrees for international students: Doctor of Juridical Sciences (SJD). https://law.ku.edu/overview-sjd. Accessed 01 Mar 2021

University of Oxford (2011) What is a DPhil? https://uni-of-oxford.custhelp.com/app/answers/detail/a_id/185/~/what-is-a-dphil%3F#:~:text=A%20DPhil%20is%20the%20Oxford,to%20write%20an%20original%20thesis. Accessed 12 Jan 2021

University of Pennsylvania Carey Law School (Online) SJD requirements. https://www.law.upenn.edu/admissions/grad/sjd/degree-requirements.php. Accessed 20 Jan 2021

University of Pittsburgh School of Law (Online) Doctor of Juridical Science (SJD) program. https://www.law.pitt.edu/centers/center-international-legal-education/doctor-juridical-science-sjd-program. Accessed 05 Mar 2021

University of Sydney Law School, What is the difference between an LLB and a JD? https://www.sydney.edu.au/law/study-law/our-law-degrees/juris-doctor.html#:~:text=The%20Juris%20Doctor%20(JD)%20is,with%20law%20degrees%20from%20overseas. Accessed 01 Feb 2021

University of Toronto Faculty of Law, Earn your law degree. https://www.law.utoronto.ca/getstarted. Accessed 05 Feb 2021

University of Washington School of Law (Online), Ph.D. in Law. https://www.law.uw.edu/academics/phd. Accessed 02 Feb 2021

Vanderbilt University Law School (2016) Ph.D. program in law and economics. https://law.vanderbilt.edu/phd/. Accessed 15 Dec 2020

Yale Law School, Ph.D. common questions: how is the Ph.D. in Law degree related to the J.S.D. degree? https://law.yale.edu/studying-law-yale/degree-programs/graduate-programs/phd-program/phd-common-questions#:~:text=Both%20are%20doctoral%20degrees%2C%20which,The%20more%20structured%20Ph.&text=Unlike%20the%20Ph.,School%2C%20not%20the%20Graduate%20School. Accessed 30 Nov 2020

Yale University Law School (Online), Ph.D. program details. https://law.yale.edu/studhying-law-yale/degree-programs/graduate-programs/phd-program/phd-program-details. Accessed 14 Feb 2021

Yale Law School, The Ph.D. in law program. https://law.yale.edu/studying-law-yale/degree-programs/graduate-programs/phd-program. Accessed 20 Jan 2021

Yale Law School, Why a Ph.D. in Law? https://law.yale.edu/studying-law-yale/degree-programs/graduate-programs/phd-program/phd-program-details. Accessed 15 Dec 2020

Ziegler AR (2020) How global should legal education be? Recommendations based on the compulsory teaching in international aspects taught at Swiss law schools. Eur J Legal Educ 1(1):49–82

Chapter 3
The Concept of the British-Styled Law Doctorate as It Obtains in the UK, the Commonwealth and Other Pertinent Jurisdictions

Abstract This chapter examines the concept of the British-styled law doctorate as it obtains in the UK, the Commonwealth and other pertinent jurisdictions, maintaining that the point of a doctorate is that it recognizes an independent contribution to the subject rather than taught coursework, however advanced. This chapter posits that Commonwealth countries have a better structured and more systematic approach to the concept of a law doctorate than the US, notwithstanding that countries such as Canada and Australia have a hybrid system of the American and British models of law doctorates.

Keywords United Kingdom (UK) · Commonwealth countries · Commonwealth Legal Education Association (CLEA) · Association of American Law Schools (AALS) · Association of Law Teachers (ALT) · Law society · British-styled law doctorate · American or US-styled law doctorates · Africa · Asia · Pacific · Latin America · Caribbean · Mediterranean · European region · Bologna process · European higher education area · Arab and European States · Juris Doctor (JD) · Post-JD · American Bar Association (ABA) · United Nations Sustainable Development Goals · Quality Assurance Agency for Higher Education · Ph.D. by thesis · Integrated Ph.D. · Professional doctorate · Ph.D. by publication · Distance learning Ph.D. · Master of Laws (LLM) · Bachelor of Laws (LLB) · Higher doctorate · Canada · Australia · New Zealand · Singapore · China

3.1 Introduction

Chapter 2 examined the concept of the American-styled law doctorate as it obtains in the US, Australia, Canada, Singapore and other pertinent jurisdictions. Analogies were also made to parallel developments in countries such as Malaysia and South Africa. Elsewhere, I have examined how law schools in the United Kingdom (UK) and in other Commonwealth countries across the world have benefitted from being members of the Commonwealth Legal Education Association (CLEA).[1] The US equivalent of CLEA is the Association of American Law Schools (AALS), though

[1] See Mwenda and Muuka (2009), p. 101. In that work, I have also highlighted other higher education bodies internationally that have several African universities as members, but those organizations do

K. K. Mwenda, *Doctoral Degree Programs in Law*,
SpringerBriefs in Law, https://doi.org/10.1007/978-3-030-88421-5_3

AALS membership is unfortunately limited only to US law schools.[2] Thus, AALS does not have as notable an international outreach as CLEA. As a national body, AALS can be best compared to the UK Association of Law Teachers (ALT) or the UK Society of Legal Scholars since both these UK bodies only have national reach.[3] It is, however, important to add that CLEA is not a regulator of bar admissions or law practice in the Commonwealth, though, through the CLEA network and platform, members can share experiences about standards of legal education. I have noted elsewhere that even the UK Law Society, the independent professional body for solicitors in the UK, does not take an approach like that of ABA's accreditation of JD degree programs in the US.[4]

In this chapter, we turn to look at the concept of the British-styled law doctorate as it obtains in the UK, the Commonwealth and other pertinent jurisdictions. An argument is made that the UK and many other Commonwealth countries have a better structured and more systematic approach to the concept of a law doctorate than the US, notwithstanding that some countries such as Canada and Australia have a hybrid system of the American and British models of law doctorates. Also, many Commonwealth countries in Africa, Asia and the Pacific region have benefited from regional treaties for the recognition of qualifications concerning higher education across nations. The following is a list of some of these treaties:

(a) Regional Convention on the Recognition of Studies, Certificates, Diplomas, Degrees and other Academic Qualifications in Higher Education in the African States 1981;
(b) Revised Convention on the Recognition of Studies, Certificates, Diplomas, Degrees and Other Academic Qualifications in Higher Education in African States 2014;
(c) Convention on the Recognition of Qualifications concerning Higher Education in the European Region 1997;
(d) Convention on the Recognition of Studies, Diplomas and Degrees concerning Higher Education in the States belonging to the Europe Region 1979;
(e) Asia-Pacific Regional Convention on the Recognition of Qualifications in Higher Education 2011; and,
(f) Regional Convention on the Recognition of Studies, Diplomas and Degrees in Higher Education in Asia and the Pacific 1983.

Closely related to developments in Commonwealth countries in Africa, Asia and the Pacific region, in Latin America and the Caribbean islands, the Regional Convention on the Recognition of Studies, Diplomas and Degrees in Higher Education in Latin America and the Caribbean, adopted in Buenos Aires on July 13, 2019, and the Regional Convention on the Recognition of Studies, Diplomas and Degrees in

---

not fall within the scope of this book (e.g. the Association of African Universities (AAU) and the Association of Commonwealth Universities (ACU)).

[2] See the Association of American Law Schools (2021), "Member schools".

[3] Mwenda and Muuka (2009), p. 102.

[4] Ibid., p. 101.

Higher Education in Latin America and the Caribbean, adopted at Mexico City on July 19, 1974, provide a similar legal framework for the recognition of qualifications concerning higher education.

Other similar regional treaties include the International Convention on the Recognition of Studies, Certificates, Diplomas and Degrees in Higher Education in the Arab and European States bordering on the Mediterranean, adopted at Nice on December 17, 1976, and the Convention on the Recognition of Studies, Diplomas and Degrees concerning Higher Education in the Arab States, adopted at Paris on December 22, 1978.

It is interesting to note that the UK has signed and ratified the Convention on the Recognition of Qualifications concerning Higher Education in the European Region 1997, known famously as the 'Lisbon Convention', whereas the US has only signed, but not ratified this treaty.[5] It is doubtful that the US has ratified any regional treaty for the recognition of qualifications concerning higher education, especially in the field of law and legal education. In contrast to the US, the UK has benefitted from developments relating to the Bologna process, a mechanism promoting intergovernmental cooperation between forty-eight (48) European countries in the field of higher education.[6] The Bologna Processstrives to bring more coherence to higher education systems across Europe.[7] The US legal education system, by contrast, does not have an international framework for the harmonization of academic standards and the structure of its law degrees, especially post-Juris Doctor (JD) degrees. As established in Chap. 2, the framework provided by the American Bar Association (ABA) is not only national in scope, but it is also limited to the JD degree only. The absence of an international framework akin to what obtains under the treaties outlined above as well as under the CLEA or the Bologna process deprives the US legal educational system of a mechanism for the internationalization of its academic standards.[8] It is, however, hoped that the US can take advantage of the framework provided for under the UNESCO Global Convention on the Recognition of Qualifications concerning Higher Education 2019, especially that this treaty was inspired by pre-existing regional treaties, such as the Lisbon Convention, and is a step in the right direction towards the implementation of the United Nations Sustainable Development Goal 4 (SDG 4). Put simply, SD 4 focusses on the enhancement of the quality

---

[5] See generally the Convention on the Recognition of Qualifications concerning Higher Education in the European Region 1997.

[6] European Higher Education Area (EHEA): "The European Higher Education Area and the Bologna Process—the United Kingdom".

[7] See the Bologna Process and the European Higher Education Area (Online), "What is the Bologna Process?".

[8] See articles appearing Online in the special edition of the *German Law Journal* dedicated to internationalization of legal education (2009), pp. 629–1168.

of higher education.[9] Indeed, as Wang, Liu and Li observe, internationalization helps elite law schools remain competitive and dominant in a rapidly changing ecology.[10]

In Europe, during the Budapest-Vienna Ministerial Conference held in March 2010, and on the occasion of the 10th anniversary of the Bologna Process, the European Higher Education Area (EHEA) was formally established[11] to facilitate student and staff mobility, to make higher education more inclusive and accessible, and to make higher education in Europe more attractive and competitive worldwide.[12] Under the Bologna Process, all participating countries, as part of the EHEA, have agreed to: (a) introduce a three-cycle higher education system consisting of bachelor's, master's and doctoral studies; (b) ensure the mutual recognition of qualifications and learning periods abroad completed at other universities; and, (c) implement a system of quality assurance, to strengthen the quality and relevance of learning and teaching.[13] The UK has been a full member of the Bologna Process/EHEA from the inception of that process in 1999.[14] The UK Quality Assurance Agency for Higher Education (QAA), the body responsible for auditing higher education institutions in the UK, adds that:

> The UK doctorate in all its forms has been confirmed as being in alignment with European-wide guidance, in particular with the Framework for Qualifications of the European Higher Education Area. This independent verification involving colleagues from non-UK European countries, as well as from the UK, recognized UK qualifications as having Europe-wide equivalence, which supports the mobility of graduates within Europe. Such mobility continues to increase through programmes such as the EU Erasmus Mundus and Marie Skłodowska-Curie initiatives, and a growing number of UK universities offer joint or jointly supervised doctoral programmes with non-UK European partner providers.[15]

Against this background, This chapter builds on the thesis that while most Commonwealth countries generally have a common approach to the concept and structure of a doctoral degree in law, the practice in the US, as already established in Chap. 2, is somewhat different.[16] In his treatise, Noble examines the origin and development of doctoral degrees and provides recommendations for the improvement of doctoral programs and degrees.[17] His work also highlights the birth of universities and doctoral degrees in medieval Europe and reviews the spread of the degree to

[9] See United Nations, Department of Economic and Social Affairs, Sustainable Development.: Goal 4—Ensure inclusive and equitable quality education and promote lifelong learning opportunities for all (2021).

[10] Wang, Liu and Li (2017).

[11] See European Higher Education Area (EHEA) (Online), "History—A Common Vision".

[12] See the Bologna Process and the European Higher Education Area (Online), "What is the Bologna Process?".

[13] Ibid.

[14] See European Higher Education Area (EHEA) (Online): "The European Higher Education Area and the Bologna Process—the United Kingdom".

[15] See UK Quality Assurance Agency for Higher Education (2020).

[16] Manley (2019), pp. 392–415.

[17] See, for instance Noble (1994).

the United States, Britain, Canada, and Australia.[18] The first doctoral degree was awarded in medieval Paris around 1150.[19] Let us now turn to look at the three main routes to a British-styled Ph.D. in Law.

3.2 The Three Main Routes to a British-Styled Ph.D. in Law

Phillips and Pugh observe that the point of a doctorate is that it recognizes an independent contribution to the subject rather than taught coursework, however advanced.[20] This observation is cardinal to our work because it sets the discussion in context on the nuances surrounding the JD, SJD, JSD and Ph.D. in Law degree programs. Indeed, it is about doctoring a philosophy in law (Ph.D.). You cannot doctor a philosophy through coursework, however advanced, although some cynics may want to argue spiritedly that coursework can also help you to 'doctor' some laws (JD) or to 'doctor' a science of law (JSD/SJD).

Indeed, many countries outside of Europe have inherited educational systems from the European countries that colonized them.[21] At independence, there was hardly any substantive transformation of the educational institutions and structures left behind by the colonialists. For example, many African francophone countries continue to mirror the educational system of France while the law schools of many Commonwealth African countries are members of CLEA, together with the UK. Indeed, many educational systems in the developing world are a carryover from colonialism.

Although the International Association of Law Schools, "a private, non-political, non-profit, volunteer, collaborative, learned society dedicated to serving the world wide legal education community" provides a global platform for legal academia to share national and international experiences on legal education, it is an association with a modest number of members, that is, just more than 160 law schools and departments from over 55 countries, representing more than 7500 law faculty members.[22] The primary mission of the International Association of Law Schools is the improvement of legal education throughout the world.[23]

> The idea for an international association of law schools emerged from several meetings of legal educators from around the world who recognized the growing inter-relationship of norms from transnational legal systems. The first such meeting was held in Florence, Italy in the year 2000, and consisted of 50 invited legal educators from twenty-seven countries. This meeting led to additional meetings of international legal educators, and during the May 2004

---

[18] Ibid.

[19] Ibid., p. 8. See also Bourner et al (2001), pp. 65–88.

[20] See Phillips and Pugh (1994), p. 181.

[21] See Britannica (Online), "Education in British colonies and former colonies".

[22] International Association of Law Schools (Online), "Who we are".

[23] Ibid.

meeting in Hawaii, 130 legal educators from forty-seven different countries unanimously adopted a resolution to form the International Association of Law Schools. In May 2005, a select group of legal educators from fourteen different countries, representing all types of the world's legal systems, gathered in Istanbul, Turkey, and agreed to the terms of a charter for the International Association of Law Schools. In October 2005, the IALS was incorporated under the laws of the District of Columbia in the United States of America.[24]

Suffice it to say, the culture of private universities and law schools is more entrenched in the US than the UK.[25] The US has more than 100 private ABA approved law schools,[26] whilst the UK only has a handful.[27] Examples of the few private law schools in the UK include the University of Law (founded in 1962 as the College of Law of England and Wales)[28] and the University of Buckingham (UB).[29] The significance of this distinction is that, in the case of the US, ABA accreditation of JD degree programs makes more sense since the industry has many private law schools. In the UK, where there are fewer private law schools, there is a lesser need for the type of accreditation of JD programs by ABA. If anything, to receive financial support from the British Government, UK public universities are expected to maintain good academic standards.[30]

In the UK, as Higginbotham observes, while most doctoral students decide to follow the Ph.D. by thesis pathway, there are five (5) viable routes to achieving this highly regarded qualification.[31] Higginbotham lists the following 5 viable routes[32]:

(a) Ph.D. by thesis;
(b) Integrated Ph.D.;
(c) Professional Doctorate;
(d) Ph.D. by publication; and,
(e) Distance learning Ph.D.

While the 5 pathways listed above are the common routes to achieving a British Ph.D. in many other disciplines,[33] for a law doctorate we can narrow it down to three (3) main routes. These three routes are the Ph.D. by thesis, the Ph.D. by publication, and the distance learning Ph.D. Let us take a more reasoned look.

---

[24] Ibid.

[25] A list of several private ABA approved law schools in the US is available at the following ABA website: https://www.americanbar.org/groups/legal_education/resources/aba_approved_law_schools/private_law_schools/. By contrast, many UK universities are public institutions and were established by royal charter, papal bull, Act of Parliament, or an instrument of government pursuant to the Further and Higher Education Act 1992 or the Higher Education and Research Act 2017.

[26] See Ibid., for the list of private ABA approved law schools in the US.

[27] See below.

[28] See the University of Law (Online).

[29] See the University of Buckingham Law School (Online).

[30] See for example UK Department of Education (2020).

[31] See Higginbotham (Online).

[32] Ibid.

[33] See UK Quality Assurance Agency for Higher Education, (2020), pp. 6–10.

3.3 Ph.D. in Law by Thesis

A Ph.D. by thesis is the most common means of getting a doctorate degree in the UK and other Commonwealth countries.[34] Describing the British Ph.D. in Law by thesis, Morris and Murphy posit that:

> In many UK law schools, the doctoral programme consists of three years of independent study culminating in a piece of writing of about 100,000 words. Students can enter the doctoral programme after completing an LLM, or in some cases, you may be allowed to enroll if you have a very high quality LLB. In some law schools, the year of enrolment will be spent in a research Masters programme which then counts towards the Ph.D. if you decide to go forward with your doctoral studies.[35]

To ensure further harmonization of standards of the British Ph.D. in Law, almost all British universities require that a Ph.D. thesis is examined by both internal and external examiners. Unlike the JSD or SJD in the US that is typically defended before a committee of faculty members within the law school where you are studying, the British Ph.D. in Law is typically examined by one internal examiner and one external examiner.[36] The external examiner will come from another university on the recommendation of your Ph.D. supervisor in consultation with you.[37] Where a Ph.D. candidate is a faculty member at the university where he or she is defending his or her Ph.D. thesis, many British universities require that both examiners be external to avoid possible bias. Such a candidate will also not have a regular Ph.D. supervisor, but simply an 'advisor' since he or she already has faculty status.[38]

In their book titled, *Getting a Ph.D. in Law*, Morris and Murphy explain the merits of getting a Ph.D. in Law and the value of the degree.[39] They go on to examine the process of preparing for the Ph.D. in Law, regarding the concept of a Ph.D. thesis, the choice of a Ph.D. topic, the types of Ph.D. programs, the choice of an institution supervisor, the making of your Ph.D. application and the securing of funding for your Ph.D. before looking at various legal research methodologies, the supervision of a Ph.D. thesis, some common problems encountered by Ph.D. students, the writing-up of a Ph.D. thesis, the examination of a Ph.D. thesis and the possibility of publishing your Ph.D. thesis or parts of it.[40] Morris and Murphy conclude their book with some recommendations of how to build a career in teaching and research, stressing the need to network and make presentations at conferences.[41]

Generally, British legal academics hardly shun their own Ph.D. in Law programs in the manner that much of US legal academia shuns American JSD or SJD degree

---

[34] Ibid., pp. 6–10.

[35] Morris and Murphy (2011), pp. 16–17.

[36] Ibid., pp. 94–97.

[37] Ibid., pp. 94–97.

[38] I obtained my Ph.D. in Law through this route and can therefore speak to the process authoritatively.

[39] See, for instance Morris and Murphy (2011), pp. 1–10.

[40] See generally, Ibid.

[41] Ibid, pp.120–132.

programs as something meant for foreign-trained lawyers.[42] Indeed, in the US, the JSD or SJD degree is like a stepchild of the family, with the JD as the favored child. By contrast, British legal academics generally hold the British Ph.D. in Law in high regard and they themselves often pursue studies for that degree. Indeed, the British Ph.D. in Law is not limited to foreigners or foreign-trained lawyers. It is designed for all legal scholars, irrespective of their country of region or where they obtained their first law degree.

It is important to stress that British law schools do not insist that you must first take a British LLM before you can be admitted to a British Ph.D. in Law program even if you already hold a relevant LLM qualification from a recognized foreign law school. As long as you have a good foreign LLB or LLM degree it can gain you admission to a British Ph.D. in Law program. Also, the prospects for admission to practice law in England if you hold a relevant foreign law degree are not as elusive as in the US.[43] This element of inclusivity in the diversity of legal traditions is what makes the British legal system more appealing internationally. Indeed, the British Ph.D. in Law is a qualification that even British law professors themselves hold. Furthermore, the British legal academy does not discriminate against American JD and SJD or JSD degrees, yet much of the US legal academy considers their own SJD or JSD degrees with suspicion. For the British, however, the internationalization of legal traditions and norms has helped to place their legal education system at the frontiers of globalization. Indeed, their legal education system is not too insular or parochial, despite major concerns about a limited presence of black minorities on the faculties of UK universities.[44] A recent 2020 report by the Guardian posits that:

> Fewer than 1% of the professors employed at UK universities are black and few British universities employ more than one or two black professors, figures show. The Higher Education Statistics Agency (Hesa) figures show UK universities continue to increase academic and non-academic staff numbers to record levels but progress on employing more staff from ethnic minorities remains sluggish.[45]

But such concerns are not unusual in the US legal academy and Ward observes that:

> After unrest escalated across the nation following the killings of George Floyd and other African Americans by police, many law schools issued solidarity and anti-racism statements. But a fair number of those institutions have few if any Black tenured professors, says Meera Deo, the author of *Unequal Profession: Race and Gender in Legal Academia*. 'We know from the little data available that there are very few tenured Black law professors in the US,' she told the ABA Journal. 'One of the key findings from my book is that the low numbers of Black tenured professors and other professors of color contribute to ongoing biases in legal academia'.[46]

---

[42] We have already established this point in Chap. 2. See Chap. 2 of this book for further discussion.

[43] See UK Solicitor Regulation Authority's (SRA) standards and regulations in regard to solicitor's qualifying exams (SQE) as well as guidelines of the UK's Bar Standards Board.

[44] See below.

[45] See, for instance, The Guardian (2020), which states that fewer than 1% of UK university professors are black.

[46] See Ward (Online).

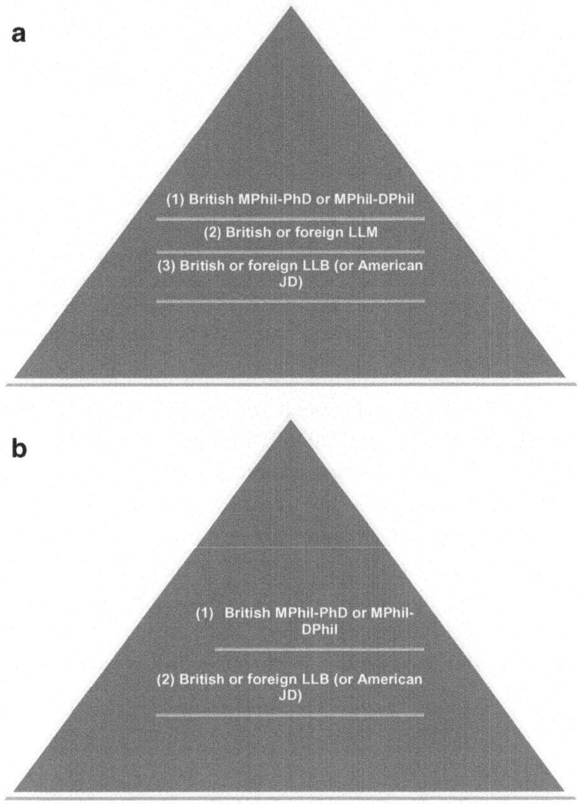

Fig. 3.1 **a** Traditional model 'A' for the British legal education system, **b** Model 'B', without an LLM, for the British legal education system

In general, the UK legal education system tries, or, at least, makes an effort, not to ostracize foreign-trained lawyers by keeping them on the margins or periphery of the industry. If you are lucky, you can even teach at a top British law school with a foreign LLB, JD, LLM or SJD degree as long as you can demonstrate your scholarly aptitude. Following below are two common typologies of routes to a law doctorate in the UK (Fig. 3.1).

3.3.1 A British View of American JSD or SJD Degree Programs

As noted above, the British legal academy does not discriminate against American JSD or SJD degrees.[47] Morris and Murphy observe that "the law Ph.D. in the US is known as the SJD or JSD (Doctor of Juridical Science), to distinguish it from the first

[47] See above.

law degree, the JD."[48] Although the JD is not considered as a terminal degree or the equivalent of a Ph.D. in Law, it is not unusual to find a US-trained lawyer with a JD or LLM serving as a law professor in the UK. Morris and Murphy contend further that:

> Many US law schools make enrolment in their LLM programmes a requirement for applying to the SJD. In some law schools, the SJD is awarded based on written work only. There are two ways of satisfying this requirement. One is identical to the traditional UK law Ph.D., requiring the production of a thesis (known in the US as a dissertation) after several years of independent study. Another way is by writing three separate articles, each of significant length and capable of being the lead article in a law review. If the second route is chosen, then the three articles usually have to be accompanied by a prefatory piece that identifies the common theme or general thesis in the articles. Some law schools offer both options, others only the dissertation option.[49]

Morris and Murphy posit further that other US law schools offer SJD programs which are a combination of coursework and writing.[50] According to Morris and Murphy, the coursework is undertaken first, and that in some schools the coursework is selected from the options offered to LLM students, while in others, students compile their own program from a combination independent reading based around certain themes and coursework.[51] A further distinction between the British Ph.D. in Law and the American JSD or SJD degree program, Morris and Murphy argue, is that in some American JSD or SJD programs you may not have a sole supervisor, but instead a dissertation committee of three or four academics who will assess your work.[52]

3.4 Ph.D. in Law by Publication

Powell observes that "the concept of having a Ph.D. submission wholly or largely based on published works has existed since the nineteenth century when in Germany it was a requirement of doctoral dissertations that they be printed and copies placed in all national university libraries."[53] Many UK law schools offer the Ph.D. by publication route whilst others do not.[54] For example, while the University of Cambridge[55] and the University of Warwick[56] offer a law Ph.D. by published work, the University of

[48] See Morris and Murphy (2011), p. 17.

[49] Ibid., p. 17.

[50] Ibid., p. 17.

[51] Ibid., p. 17.

[52] Ibid., p. 17.

[53] See Powell (2004), p.7–14.

[54] On the increase in the use of publications in doctoral submissions at British universities, see Ibid., p. 12.

[55] The University of Cambridge Ph.D. by special regulations (Online).

[56] See below.

Oxford does not. Higginbotham argues that the Ph.D. by publication route generally involves submitting previously published work—such as books, book chapters or journal articles, which together form a coherent body of work and show evidence of an original contribution to a particular field of study.[57] In the UK, this route to a doctoral degree is common amongst some mid-career academics who did not have a chance to pursue their Ph.D..[58] Such academics often pursue the 'retrospective option' of obtaining a Ph.D. by submitting already published work.[59]

The University of Bristol observes that "a Ph.D. by published work allows you to apply for a research degree based on work you have already had published, as opposed to work undertaken as a student of the University."[60] Similarly, the Institute of Development Studies in the UK posits that its program for 'the Ph.D. by Published Works in Development Studies is awarded to candidates who have already completed original and significant research in the field of development studies and have a coherent body of published works, but who have not had the opportunity to undertake a research programme leading to a Ph.D..'[61] And the Institute of Development Studies maintains that "the portfolio of research you submit for this Ph.D. will be of the same quality, rigor and volume as a typical Ph.D.."[62] Be that as it may, Badley argues that "there is still a lack of commonality in higher education about the nature of the Ph.D. by published work," and that "one way of gaining greater commonality would be to strengthen the use of the critical appraisal as an academic text which also should be required to meet the admittedly problematical standards of publishability."[63]

The other option in the UK for a Ph.D. by publication is the 'prospective option' where an academic publishes new work incrementally for a Ph.D. by publication.[64] However, a Ph.D. by publication (or published work) should not be confused with a higher or senior doctorate.[65] We will examine the concept of a higher doctorate in Chap. 4. Suffice it to say, the Ph.D. by publication route is not unusual in many British law schools.[66] This route is actually similar to the writing of three separate articles at a US law school for the JSD or SJD degree, each of significant length and capable of being the lead article in a law review.[67] As in the case of the SJD or JSD degree, the British Ph.D. by publication route is usually accompanied by a prefatory piece (i.e. the critical appraisal) that identifies the common theme or general thesis in the articles.[68] Higginbotham observes that,

---

[57] See Higginbotham (Online).

[58] Ibid.

[59] See Smith (2015), pp. 24–31.

[60] The University of Bristol (Online), "Ph.D. by published work".

[61] Institute of Development Studies (Online), "Ph.D. in Development Studies by Published Work".

[62] See Ibid.

[63] Badley (2009), pp. 331–342.

[64] Smith (2015), pp. 24–31.

[65] See generally Powell and Crouch (2008).

[66] See generally, for example Christianson, et al (2015), pp. 69–85 and Green and Powell (2005).

[67] See above.

[68] See Smith (2015), pp. 81–118.

> Generally, a minimum of five to eight published pieces are required, but this varies between institutions and depends on their length. The published work will be assessed to the same rigorous standards as a traditional Ph.D. by thesis. You must also provide a written supporting statement, which can range from 5,000 to 20,000 words, and present your work to an academic committee. A supervisor will assist you with selecting which publications to submit and with the supporting statement.[69]

There is, however, a caveat in many admission requirements for the Ph.D. by publication. Some universities accept only their own graduates for a Ph.D. by publication, while others restrict this route to their academic staff.[70] In general, as Higginbotham observes, you should have graduated from your first degree at least seven years ago to be eligible.[71] The University of Warwick, for example, provides that a Ph.D. by publication is "a Ph.D. awarded for the submission of a portfolio of published research to the standard of a regular Ph.D.", and that candidates should be either Warwick academic staff, Warwick administrative staff or Warwick library staff who have been employed at Warwick for at least three years immediately prior to the submission of the published work, or graduates of any internationally recognized university of at least seven year's standing normally holding a Bachelor's degree or equivalent.[72]

Be that as it may, a major criticism of the Ph.D. by publication route, notwithstanding dictates of the Vancouver Protocol on the attribution of coauthored work,[73] relates to how to treat coauthored work when it is submitted as part of the portfolio of published work for the Ph.D. award. Indeed, what fraction of the co-authored work can be attributed to the Ph.D. candidate? And how can we determine the accuracy of this quantification? Equally important is how to treat a book edited and submitted for a Ph.D. by publication if such a book contains mainly papers presented by several scholars at an academic conference. What fraction of this book can be attributed to the Ph.D. candidate's own work?

A related criticism of the Ph.D. by publication route is the view postulated by Professor Wilson that, "in spite of the requirement that the award of a Ph.D. by published work and by a conventional thesis should achieve comparability of standards [the question of how many publications] probably leads to an overestimate of the number of publications required for the published work route."[74] Furthermore, we would be pursuing a red herring to try to advocate for a sacrosanct rule that predetermines the type of law journals or law reviews in which articles submitted for

---

[69] See, for instance, Higginbotham (Online), *op. cit.*

[70] See Ibid.

[71] See Ibid.

[72] See the University of Warwick (Online), "Ph.D. by published work".

[73] *Cf.* Smith (2015), p. 66–67 argues that: "The Vancouver Protocol is internationally recognized as the standard for determining authorship on publications. It was first described by the International Committee of Medical Journal Ethics and is now applied across all disciplines in the world's top universities. The updated Vancouver protocols (ICMJE, 2013) for co-authorship state that authorship credit should be based on all the following criteria: Substantial contributions to conception and design, acquisition of data, or analysis and interpretation of data; Drafting the article and revising it critically for important intellectual content; and; Final approval of the version to be published".

[74] Powell (2004), p. 25.

a Ph.D. by publication should have been published. Indeed, different countries and different institutions have different standards for the publication of journal articles.

3.5 Distance Learning Ph.D. in Law

Reflecting on the impact of the coronavirus (COVID-19) pandemic and the consequent restrictions to visiting university campuses in the UK, Higginbotham argues that there is now a greater need for students to carry out their doctoral research at home, wherever possible.[75] According to Higginbotham, the impact of the pandemic has meant an increase in the number of online Ph.D.s available from UK institutions.[76] Even before the pandemic started, a few leading UK law schools had already embarked on the option of a Ph.D. in Law by distance learning.[77] The University of Birmingham School of Law, for example, has been offering a Ph.D. in Law by distance learning, and submits that:

> A Ph.D. by Distance Learning allows you to undertake the majority of your research at an off-campus location. You are therefore able to do the research required for your Ph.D. in a location of your choosing; only making one annual visit to the University.[78]

The University of Glasgow School of Law in Scotland also offers a Ph.D. in Law by distance learning, stressing that the program is "without attendance at the University of Glasgow".[79] Closely related to this, the University of Leicester School of Law offers a Ph.D. in Law by distance learning as well.[80]

Higginbotham contends that since the traditional Ph.D. route in the UK is based primarily on independent research rather than time spent in lectures and seminars, distance learning is a viable route for many Ph.D. students and that:

> For the most part, you'll be in touch with your supervisor by phone, email or Skype/Zoom. However, even if you opt for this form of research, you'll generally still need to attend university for one or two weeks of each academic year for meetings and to receive research skills training. Your final examination may be undertaken either face-to-face or virtually. With distance learning Ph.D.s, you can usually register as a full or part-time student. The level of fees you pay varies between institutions – some charge the same as for a standard Ph.D. while others offer a reduced rate.[81]

In the US, once an SJD or JSD student satisfies the residency requirements of the program, he or she is allowed to continue writing his or her SJD or JSD dissertation by 'distance learning', with occasional visits, if necessary, to the law school.[82] The

---

[75] Higginbotham (Online).

[76] Ibid.

[77] See below.

[78] See University of Birmingham School of Law (Online), "Law Ph.D. by Distance Learning".

[79] See University of Glasgow School of Law (Online), "Ph.D. by Distance".

[80] See University of Leicester Law School (Online) "Research degrees: Law—Ph.D., MPhil.

[81] Higginbotham (Online).

[82] See below.

University Michigan Law School, for example, has a one-year residency requirement for SJD students.[83] Similarly, the University of Pennsylvania Carey Law School stipulates that 'All SJD students are required to spend the first full academic year of their SJD program in residence at the Law School.'[84]

Following below are two models of a British-styled doctorate that mirror closely the American-styled model of a law doctorate but which, however, do not lead a law doctorate in the UK and many other parts of the Commonwealth. These two models lead to doctoral degrees in fields outside law.

3.6 The Integrated Ph.D. Model

Not many British law schools have warmed up to the integrated Ph.D. model. In the UK, this Ph.D. model is found mainly in fields outside law. In general, the British integrated Ph.D. model can be said to be akin to the American JSD or SJD degree programs that combine coursework and writing.[85] Given that in the US a Ph.D. in a cognate field is an attractive qualification for those aspiring to be law teachers, some law professors with Ph.D.s in cognate fields could have arguably brought in methodologies from those disciplines to bear on the study of law.

Higginbotham points out that the British integrated Ph.D. model, also known as the '1+3 model'[86] or the 'New Route Ph.D.', is a four-year qualification involving a one-year research Masters degree before progressing onto a three-year Ph.D.[87] Offered by a select number of universities across the UK, integrated Ph.D.s, Higginbotham posits, are supported by the British Government and the British Council, and they expose you to a combination of taught materials, practical experience and advanced research.[88]

3.7 Professional Doctorate

Like the British integrated Ph.D. model, the British professional doctorate model is found mainly in fields outside law. The concept of a professional law doctorate in the UK is still alien. That said, many professional doctoral programs include a significant taught component and a smaller research project.[89] A good example of a professional doctorate is the degree of Doctor of Business Administration (DBA) which differs

[83] See University of Michigan Law School (Online), "Admission to the SJD Program".

[84] See University of Pennsylvania Carey Law School (Online), "SJD Requirements—First Year".

[85] Morris and Murphy (2011), p. 17.

[86] Ibid., p. 17.

[87] Higginbotham (Online).

[88] Ibid.

[89] See Ibid.

from a Ph.D. by thesis in Business Administration. Also, the degree of Doctor of Education (Ed.D.) is considered by many as a professional doctorate, as opposed to a Ph.D. in Education.[90] Increasingly, the EdD is being offered by many universities in the UK and the US as a part-time or Online doctoral degree program.[91] In the US, as we saw in Chap. 2, the JD degree is also at times treated as a professional doctorate akin to the Doctor of Medicine (MD) degree. But this view of the JD, as already established,[92] is not free from illogical difficulty.

Let us now turn to examine the blend or hybrid model of the American and British-styled approaches to the concept of a law doctorate.

3.8 Hybrid Approaches to the Concept of a Law Doctorate in Canada, Australia, New Zealand, Singapore and Other Pertinent Jurisdictions, Including China

Chapter 2, we established that some universities in Canada, Australia and Singapore have adopted the American styled-JD degree. Writing on developments in Canada, Monahan observed in a 2006 article that,

> In an effort to have their degrees better understood and more marketable internationally, a growing number of Canadian law schools are switching from the traditional LLB designation to the American-style JD... Canadian law school deans said that while the LLB – which stands for *legum baccalaureus* or bachelor of laws in Latin – is a second-entry degree (i.e. in Canada) just like the JD – juris doctor or doctor of laws – not all recruiters or law firms outside of Canada understand that. As a result, some think it's an undergraduate degree or are confused about what it is.[93]

Monahan continued:

> Even outside the United States, having a degree that is understood globally opens more doors in today's globalized legal world. 'There is a feeling that, increasingly, as our students market themselves internationally, the JD designation will give them better opportunity to market themselves and that it is a more accurate reflection of what their actual degree is…'.[94]

Canada has a dual system of common law and civil law traditions.[95] *Canada's legal system is based on the English and French systems.*[96] So, some Canadian law schools offer instruction in the common law and have adopted the American styled-JD whereas others offer instruction in the civil law have retained the LLB or the Bachelor of Civil Law (BCL) designations. Then, there are also those that offer

---

[90] See Ibid.

[91] See Ibid.

[92] See above. See also generally the discussion in Chap. 2.

[93] See York University Osgoode Hall Law School (Online).

[94] See Ibid.

[95] See Canada's Department of Justice (Online).

[96] See Ibid.

dual programs.[97] Canada provides an example of how the legal traditions of the neighboring country, the US, have influenced the adoption of the JD. At the same time, the lingering influence of the Commonwealth and some civil law traditions has left pockets of the LLB still present in Canada. The story of Canada becomes even more interesting when we move to the research doctorate in law. The University of Toronto is the only university in Canada that has adopted the American-styled SJD program.[98] Other Canadian law schools have retained the Ph.D. in Law model, with McGill University retaining its Doctor of Civil Law (DCL) degree[99] as the equivalent of the Ph.D. in Law. Indeed, Canada takes a hybrid approach to the concept of a law doctorate.

Unlike SJD or JSD programs in the US that require applicants to those programs to complete a US LLM before being admitted as SJD or JSD students, the Canadian SJD program at the University of Toronto, like a British Ph.D. in Law program, will admit candidates with a good foreign LLB or LLM degree from a recognized foreign university.[100] According to the University of Toronto Faculty of Law,

> Applicants to the SJD Direct-Entry program who have achieved a minimum A- average in their Bachelor of Laws (LLB) or Juris Doctor (JD), and have demonstrated, through substantive writing, their ability to engage in and generate high-level thought and quality research, may be considered for Direct-Entry into the SJD program (i.e., admission to the SJD program without having completed a LLM degree).[101]

Again, we see here elements of a hybrid approach to the law doctorate in Canada. Parallel developments can be seen in Australia where some universities now offer the JD and SJD degree programs whilst others offer the LLB and Ph.D. in Law. To illustrate, the University of New South Wales, Flinders University, the University of Sydney, the University of Western Australia, and the University of Melbourne are some leading universities in Australia that offer the American-styled JD degree.[102] In Chap. 2, we noted that the University of Sydney postulates that both the JD and LLB lead to professional accreditation to practice law in Australia and that the LLB is for those commencing law studies from high school while the JD is for those who already have a degree.[103] Then, there are also Australian universities that maintain both the JD and LLB degree programs.[104] Examples of Australian universities that offer both

---

[97] McGill University Faculty of Law, for example, offers both the JD and BCL first professional law degrees. See McGill University Faculty of Law (Online), "Our BCL/JD Program in Law".

[98] See University of Toronto Faculty of Law (Online), "Doctor of Juridical Science (SJD) Admissions".

[99] See McGill University Faculty of Law (Online), "Doctoral Program".

[100] See below.

[101] See University of Toronto Faculty of Law (Online), "Doctor of Juridical Science (SJD) Admissions".

[102] See the website of each of these Australian law schools for information on the JD degree program.

[103] See the University of Sydney Law School (Online), "What's the difference between an LLB and a JD?".

[104] See below.

the JD and LLB include the Australian National University, Bond University, Deakin University, Griffith University, and Monash University.[105]

Bond University Faculty of Law draws a distinction between its JD and LLB degree programs, stating that:

> The Juris Doctor prepares students for a career as a legal professional, both within Australia and overseas. It is an alternative to the Bachelor of Laws for students who have completed an undergraduate degree in any discipline.[106]

With the strong ties that exist between Bond University Faculty of Law and some Canadian institutions,[107] it is easy to see how the motivations of many Canadian law schools, as pointed out by Monahan above,[108] to switch to the JD degree program have influenced the development of the Australian JD degree program at Bond University. Interestingly, Bond University Faculty of Law not only runs both the LLB and JD programs, but also both the SJD and Ph.D. in Law programs.[109] Distinguishing the SJD from the Ph.D. in Law, Bond University Faculty of Law submits that:

> The Doctor of Legal Science (Research) is an industry and professional focused program which combines course and thesis work in an area of legal discipline that is of interest to you, providing you with the opportunity to deepen your research skills and knowledge in an area of the law... The Doctor of Legal Science (Research) (SJD) is a higher degree by research program awarded for a combination of coursework followed by a 50,000 word thesis[110]

In regard to its Ph.D. in Law program, Bond University states as follows:

> The Doctor of Philosophy (Ph.D.) must be significant original research. During the course of the degree the candidate will further develop their specialist knowledge and have deep methodological capacity. Depending on the field of specialisation, the degree culminates in an 80,000-word thesis. A Doctor of Philosophy is an internationally recognised research degree and is a pathway to an academic or research career.[111]

The two statements above from Bond University Faculty of Law draw a clear distinction between the SJD and Ph.D. in Law. Indeed, a Ph.D. in Law from Bond University, rather than an SJD, is the law doctorate that is considered as a more 'serious' doctorate for purposes of pursuing an academic career.[112] The SJD, by contrast, is focused on industry outside academia.

Closely related to the Bond University SJD program, the SJD program at the University of Western Australia is also structured along similar lines, with both coursework and research.[113] As the University of Western Australia observes:

---

[105] See the website of each of these Australian law schools for information on the JD and LLB degree programs.

[106] See Bond University Faculty of Law (Online), "Juris Doctor.

[107] See Ibid.

[108] See above.

[109] See below.

[110] See, for instance, Bond University Faculty of Law (Online), "Study a Doctor of Legal Science (Research) in Australia.

[111] See, for instance, Bond University Faculty of Law (Online), "Doctor of Philosophy".

[112] See above.

[113] See below.

> The Doctor of Juridical Science is a special opportunity to gain distinguished professional recognition for high quality research. With both a coursework and thesis component, this professional doctorate recognizes a distinguished original contribution to professional knowledge… It involves completion of a combination of coursework units and a 50,000 to 60,000 word thesis.[114]

Indeed, the University of Western Australia makes it clear that the SJD program there leads to a professional doctorate, not an academic doctorate.[115] Bond University, the University of Western Australia, the Australian National University, La Trobe University, the University of Canberra, the University of New South Wales, the University of Sydney, the University of Technology Sydney, and the University of Western Australia are some of the Australian universities that offer the SJD program,[116] although others like Bond also offer an option for a Ph.D. in Law.[117]

In general, there are more law schools in Australia that offer the Ph.D. in Law program than the SJD program.[118] The Australian version of the SJD program has, however, caught up at the University of Waikato in New Zealand,[119] although Waikato, like Bond, also offers a Ph.D. in Law program.[120] There is hardly any noticeable JD program in New Zealand. The LLB remains the most prominent first professional law degree there. Otherwise, many leading universities in Australia and New Zealand offer the Ph.D. in Law, as opposed to the JSD or SJD, despite both the Australian and New Zealand legal education systems showing elements of a hybrid approach to the concept of a law doctorate.[121]

Similarly, in Singapore, while the National University of Singapore offers both the LLB and JD degree programs, it does not offer the SJD or JSD program.[122] Rather, it offers a Ph.D. in Law program.[123] In China, by mid-2014, the JD program was being offered at the University of Hong Kong, the City University of Hong Kong, and the Chinese University of Hong Kong.[124] Also, a number of Chinese universities have been quick to adopt the American-styled SJD degree program.[125] For example, Tsinghua University Law School in Beijing,[126] KoGuan Law School at Shanghai Jiao

---

[114] See, for example, the University of Western Australia (Online), "Doctor of Juridical Science".

[115] See Ibid.

[116] See the websites of each of these Australian law schools for information on the SJD program.

[117] See above.

[118] See International Education Specialists (Online), "IDP Australia—Doctorate Law and Legal Studies courses".

[119] See the University of Waikato (Online), "Doctor of Juridical Science".

[120] See the University of Waikato (Online), "Doctor of Philosophy (Law)".

[121] See International Education Specialists (Online), "IDP Australia—Doctorate Law and Legal Studies courses".

[122] See National University of Singapore Faculty of Law (Online), "Research degrees—Doctor of Philosophy (Ph.D.)".

[123] See Ibid.

[124] See MayForbes (Online), "How Prestigious is the Juris Doctor?" *South China Morning Post.*

[125] See below.

[126] See for instance Tsinghua University Law School (Online), "Doctor of Juridical Science (SJD)".

Tong University in Shanghai,[127] and Guanghua Law School at Zhejiang University in Hangzhou[128] offer SJD degree program. Wang, Liu and Li contend that:

> At the turn of the twenty-first century, legal education in China exploded. Driven by the state-led expansion of higher education, the number of law schools rapidly increased from less than 200 in the 1990s to over 600 in 2006. The total number of law graduates also surged, from 31,500 in 1999 to 208,000 in 2008. In the meantime, Chinese law schools, especially the elite ones, became increasingly interested in sending students to study abroad, recruiting new faculty members with foreign law degrees, launching new journals in English, and developing student and scholar exchange programs with foreign institutional partners.[129]

According to Wang, Liu and Li, while the domestic consequences of China's legal education expansion have been well-documented, these efforts on internationalization have largely been overlooked in the existing literature on Chinese legal education.[130] Looking at the causes, strategies, and implications of elite Chinese law schools' internationalization, the three authors argue that efforts of Chinese law schools towards global convergence should be understood primarily as their response to domestic challenges and peer pressures.[131] Wang, Liu and Li maintain that it is these challenges and pressures that have led elite Chinese law schools to recruit more faculty members with international backgrounds and produce more law graduates with global orientations.[132] They posit further that:

> Internationalization helps elite law schools remain competitive and dominant in the rapidly changing ecology of Chinese legal education. Meanwhile, it also presents opportunities for international law schools to further explore the potential of the legal education market in China.[133]

In the US, the Center on the Legal Profession at Harvard University Law School, in an article titled, '*An American Degree Goes Global: The transformation of the Doctorate of Science and Law*', posits that "the most advanced law degrees at elite law schools in the United States are the JSD (Doctor of the Science of Law) and the SJD (Doctor of Juridical Science)" and that "these degrees are primarily awarded to foreign law students."[134] Harvard's Center on the Legal Profession then goes on to say that most US law professors do not have a JSD or SJD, but rather a JD and sometimes a Ph.D. from another field.[135] The Center asks an important question for

---

[127] See KoGuan Law School, Shanghai Jiao Tong University (Online), "SJD Program".

[128] See Guanghua Law School, Zhejiang University (Online), "Master of Laws (LLM) and Doctor of Juridical Science (SJD) in Chinese Law".

[129] See for instance, Wang, Liu and Li (2017), p. 237.

[130] Ibid., pp. 237–238.

[131] Ibid., p. 238.

[132] Ibid., p. 238.

[133] See Ibid., p. 238.

[134] Center on the Legal Profession, Harvard University Law School (2015)—An American Degree Goes Global: The transformation of the Doctorate of Science and Law.

[135] See Ibid.

anyone reading this book to think about, that is, "why is it that the JSD. and SJD are offered primarily to foreigners, not Americans?".[136]

3.9 Conclusion

This chapter has examined the concept of the British-styled law doctorate as it obtains in the UK, the Commonwealth and other pertinent jurisdictions, with analogies drawn from developments in North America, Asia and the Pacific. Our findings show that no law school in the UK offers the American-styled SJD or JSD program and that UK law schools offer the Ph.D. in Law as a terminal degree.[137] The chapter noted that the point of a doctorate is that it recognizes an independent contribution to the subject rather than taught coursework, however advanced. To draw distinctions between the British Ph.D. in Law and the American SJD or JSD programs, we proceeded to examine developments in countries that offer both the Ph.D. in Law and the SJD or JSD program and those that offer only the Ph.D. in Law or the SJD/JSD only. We found that many law schools in Canada, Australia, New Zealand, and Singapore offer the Ph.D. in Law, not the SJD or JSD. We also looked at the spirited efforts of many Chinese law schools to adopt American-styled law degrees as a quest to internationalize.

The UK and many other Commonwealth countries, we observed, have a better structured and more systematic approach to the concept of a law doctorate than the US, notwithstanding that countries such as Canada and Australia have a hybrid system of the American and British models of law doctorates. It was also pointed that the UK and many Commonwealth countries in Africa, Asia and the Pacific region have benefited from regional treaties for the recognition of qualifications concerning higher education as well as from being members of CLEA. The UK has also benefitted from developments relating to the Bologna process that bring more coherence to higher education systems across Europe. The US legal education system, by contrast, and as already established above, does not have the equivalent of the Bologna process or regional treaties for the recognition of qualifications concerning higher education, especially in regard to post-JD degrees. Such shortcomings, we concluded, deprive the US legal academy of a mechanism to help internationalize its academic standards. As a result, many post-JD programs remain largely less competitive and less attractive internationally. The uncertainty surrounding the recognition of post-JD qualifications in the US and elsewhere often impacts negatively on the prospects for mobility and employability of the degree-holder.

---

[136] See Ibid.

[137] Mindful, of course, that many law schools in the UK and other Commonwealth countries have provision for a higher doctorate that ranks substantially higher than a Ph.D. in Law. We will examine the concept of a higher doctorate in the next chapter.

References

American Bar Association, Private Law Schools in the US. https://www.americanbar.org/groups/legal_education/resources/aba_approved_law_schools/private_law_schools/. Accessed 2 Mar 2021

Association of American Law Schools (2021) Member schools. https://www.aals.org/member-schools/. Accessed 2 Mar 2021

Badley G (2009) Publish and be doctor-rated: the Ph.D. by published work. Quality Assur Educ 17(4):331–342

Bologna Process and the European Higher Education Area, What is the Bologna Process? https://ec.europa.eu/education/policies/higher-education/bologna-process-and-european-higher-education-area_en. Accessed on 4 Aug 2021

Bond University Faculty of Law, Doctor of Philosophy. https://bond.edu.au/intl/program/doctor-philosophy. Accessed 15 Mar 2021

Bond University Faculty of Law, Juris Doctor. https://bond.edu.au/intl/program/juris-doctor. Accessed 2 Mar 2021

Bond University Faculty of Law, Study a Doctor of Legal Science (Research) in Australia. https://bond.edu.au/intl/program/doctor-legal-science-research. Accessed 10 Mar 2021

Bourner T, Bowden R, Laing S (2001) Professional doctorates in England. Stud High Educ 26(1):65–88

Britannica, Education in British colonies and former colonies. https://www.britannica.com/topic/education/Education-in-British-colonies-and-former-colonies. Accessed 12 Mar 2021

Canada's Department of Justice, Where our legal system comes from. https://www.justice.gc.ca/eng/csj-sjc/just/03.html. Accessed 4 Mar 2021

Center on the Legal Profession, Harvard University Law School (2015) An American degree goes global: the transformation of the doctorate of science and law. The Practice 1(5). https://thepractice.law.harvard.edu/article/an-american-degree-goes-global/. Accessed 20 Feb 2021

Christianson B, Elliott M, Massey B (2015) The role of publications and other artifacts in submissions for the UK Ph.D.. Council for Graduate Education, Lichfield, UK

Convention on the recognition of qualifications concerning higher education in the European Region 1997. https://www.coe.int/en/web/conventions/full-list/-/conventions/treaty/165/signatures?p_auth=vAIJiWTK. Accessed on 4 Jun 2021

Council of Europe, Chart of signatures and ratifications of treaty 165—Convention on the recognition of qualifications concerning higher education in the European Region: status as of 16/02/2021. https://www.coe.int/en/web/conventions/full-list/-/conventions/treaty/165/signatures?p_auth=vAIJiWTK. Accessed 16 Feb 2021

European Higher Education Area (EHEA), History—a common vision. http://www.ehea.info/pid34248/history.html. Accessed 28 Jan 2021

European Higher Education Area (EHEA), The European higher education area and the Bologna process—the United Kingdom. http://www.ehea.info/page-united-kingdom. Accessed 2 Jan 2021

German Law Journal (2009) 10(6/7). https://germanlawjournal.com/wp-content/uploads/GLJ_Vol_10_No_07.pdf. Accessed 21 Jan 2021

Green H, Powell S (2005) Doctoral study in contemporary higher education. Open University Press, Maidenhead

Guanghua Law School, Zhejiang University, A farewell to our LLM and SJD students 2019. http://www.ghls.zju.edu.cn/ghlscn/2019/0708/c13699a1291308/page.htm. Accessed 22 Mar 2021

Guanghua Law School, Zhejiang University, Master of Laws (LLM) and Doctor of Juridical Science (SJD) in Chinese Law. https://cpb-ap-se2.wpmucdn.com/blog.une.edu.au/dist/a/1215/files/2015/04/Zhejiang-University-LL.M-SJD-English-Program-in-Chinese-Law-2015.pdf. Accessed 22 Mar 2021

Higginbotham D (2020) 5 Routes to getting a doctorate. https://www.prospects.ac.uk/postgraduate-study/phd-study/5-routes-to-getting-a-doctorate. Accessed 20 Jan 2020

Institute of Development Studies, Ph.D. in development studies by published work. https://www.ids.ac.uk/learn-at-ids/phd-by-published-works/. Accessed 2 Mar 2021
International Association of Law Schools, Who we are. https://www.ialsnet.org/. Accessed 5 Mar 2021
International Education Specialists, IDP Australia—Doctorate Law and Legal Studies courses. https://www.idp.com/australia/search/law-and-legal-studies/doctorate/. Accessed 12 Mar 2021
KoGuan Law School, Shanghai Jiao Tong University, SJD Program. https://law.sjtu.edu.cn/International/Article120111.aspx. Accessed 2 Mar 2021
Manley S (2019) Degree (un)equivalencies: the confounding case of the Juris doctor. J Leg Educ 68(2):392–415
MayForbes C (2014) How prestigious is the Juris doctor? South China Morning Post. https://www.scmp.com/article/1539477/how-prestigious-juris-doctor. Accessed 2 Mar 2021
McGill University Faculty of Law, Doctoral Program. https://www.mcgill.ca/law/grad-studies/doctoral-program. Accessed 3 Mar 2021
McGill University Faculty of Law, Our BCL/JD program in law. https://www.mcgill.ca/law/bcl-jd. Accessed 2 Mar 2021
Morris C, Murphy C (2011) Getting a Ph.D. in Law. Hart Publishing, Oxford and Portland, OR
Mwenda KK, Muuka GN (2009) Developing academic programs in Commonwealth African Law schools: lessons from the British and American Legal Education Systems. In: Mwenda KK, Muuka GN (eds) The challenge of change in Africa's Higher Education in the 21st Century. Cambria Press, Amherst, NY
National University of Singapore Faculty of Law, Research degrees—Doctor of Philosophy (Ph.D.). https://law1.nus.edu.sg/admissions/research_prog.html. Accessed 23 Jan 2021
Noble KA (1994) Changing doctoral degrees: an international perspective, (Society for Research into Higher Education). Open University Press, Buckingham, UK
Peacock S (2017) The Ph.D. by publication. Int J Dr Stud 12:123–134
Phillips EM, Pugh DS (1994) How to get a Ph.D. Open University Press, Buckingham
Powell (2004) The award of Ph.D. by published work in the UK. UK Council for Graduate Education, Lichfield
Powell S, Crouch N (2008) Higher doctorate awards in the UK. UK Council for Graduate Education, Lichfield
Smith S (2015) Ph.D. by published work: a practical guide for success. Palgrave, London
Ward SF (2020) How many tenured law professors are Black? Public data does not say. ABA J. https://www.abajournal.com/web/article/how-many-tenured-law-professors-are-black-public-data-does-not-say. Accessed on 2 Mar 2021
The Bologna Process and the European Higher Education Area, What is the Bologna Process? https://ec.europa.eu/education/policies/higher-education/bologna-process-and-european-higher-education-area_en. Accessed 1 Mar 2021
The Guardian (2020) Fewer than 1% of UK university professors are black, figures show. https://www.theguardian.com/education/2020/feb/27/fewer-than-1-of-uk-university-professors-are-black-figures-show. Accessed 27 July 2021
The University of Law. https://www.law.ac.uk/. Accessed 1 Mar 2021
The University of Warwick, Ph.D. by published work. https://warwick.ac.uk/study/postgraduate/research/phdbypublishedwork. Accessed 21 Jan 2021
The University of Western Australia, Doctor of Juridical Science. https://www.uwa.edu.au/study/courses/doctor-of-juridical-science. Accessed 16 Jan 2021
Tsinghua University Law School, Doctor of Juridical Science (SJD). https://school.cucas.cn/Tsinghua-University-257/program/Juridical-Sciences--S-J-D---31503.html. Accessed 2 Mar 2021
UK Department of Education (2020) Government scheme to help universities in financial difficulties: new government scheme launched to support English universities at risk of insolvency. https://www.gov.uk/government/news/government-scheme-to-help-universities-in-financial-difficulties. Accessed 9 Feb 2021

UK Quality Assurance Agency for Higher Education (2020) Characteristics statement—doctoral degree. https://www.qaa.ac.uk/docs/qaa/quality-code/doctoral-degree-characteristics-statement-2020.pdf?sfvrsn=a3c5ca81_14. Accessed 1 Mar 2021

United Nations, Department of Economic and Social Affairs, Sustainable Development: Goal 4—ensure inclusive and equitable quality education and promote lifelong learning opportunities for all. https://sdgs.un.org/goals/goal4. Accessed 1 Mar 2021

University of Birmingham School of Law, Law Ph.D. by distance learning. https://www.birmingham.ac.uk/postgraduate/courses/research/arts-law-inter/law-phd-distance-learning.aspx. Accessed 1 Feb 2021

University of Bristol, Ph.D. by published work. https://www.bristol.ac.uk/students/support/finances/tuition-fees/pgr/phd-by-published-work/. Accessed 19 Jan 2021

University of Buckingham Law School. https://www.buckingham.ac.uk/law. Accessed 12 Mar 2021

University of Cambridge, Ph.D. by special regulations. https://www.cambridgestudents.cam.ac.uk/your-course/examinations/graduate-exam-information/higher-degrees/phd-special-regulations. Accessed 2 Mar 2021

University of Glasgow School of Law, Ph.D. by distance. https://www.gla.ac.uk/schools/law/postgraduateresearch/phd-by-distance/. Accessed 1 Feb 2021

University of Leicester Law School, Research degrees: Law—Ph.D., M.Phil. https://le.ac.uk/study/research-degrees/research-subjects/law. Accessed 5 Mar 2021

University of Michigan Law School, Admission to the SJD Program. https://www.law.umich.edu/prospectivestudents/graduate/degreeprograms/sjd/Pages/sjdadmission.aspx. Accessed 30 Dec 2020

University of Pennsylvania Carey Law School, SJD requirements—first year. https://www.law.upenn.edu/admissions/grad/sjd/degree-requirements.php. Accessed 1 Mar 2021

University of Sydney Law School, What's the difference between an LLB and a JD? https://www.sydney.edu.au/law/study-law/our-law-degrees/juris-doctor.html. Accessed 5 Mar 2021

University of Toronto Faculty of Law, Doctor of Juridical Science (SJD) Admissions. https://www.law.utoronto.ca/admissions/graduate-admissions/sjd-admissions. Accessed 30 Jan 2021

University of Waikato, Doctor of Juridical Science. https://www.waikato.ac.nz/study/qualifications/doctor-of-juridical-science. Accessed 5 Mar 2021

University of Waikato, Doctor of Philosophy (Law). https://www.waikato.ac.nz/study/qualifications/doctor-of-philosophy-law. Accessed 5 Mar 2021

Wang Z, Liu S, Li X (2017) Internationalizing Chinese legal education in the early twenty-first century. J Leg Educ 66(2):237–238

York University Osgoode Law School, Dean Patrick Monahan on the growing number of Canadian Law Schools switching from the LLB to JD degree designation. https://web.archive.org/web/20080610142423/http://osgoode.yorku.ca/media2.nsf/83303ffe5af03ed585256ae6005379c9/ef8025cc6549271e852574200056fcc8%21OpenDocument. Accessed 21 Jan 2021

Chapter 4
Beyond the Ph.D.

Abstract This chapter introduces the concept of a higher doctorate as a qualification that stands *substantially* higher than a Ph.D. at many leading universities in the Commonwealth. Also, this chapter distinguishes higher doctorates from a Ph.D. and postdoctoral fellowship, contending that the concept of a higher doctorate is a more objective benchmark for making faculty appointments to full professorship than the not-so-clear criteria at some law schools.

Keywords Higher doctorate · Doctorat dÉtat (i.e. 'State doctorate') · Doctorat de troisième cycle (i.e. 'postgraduate doctorate') · Habilitation · Doktorgrad (i.e. 'dr. phil.') · Doktor nauk · Australia · Austria · Liechtenstein · Switzerland · Poland · Russia · Germany · France · Danish · United Kingdom · Canada · United States (US) · American-styled JD · American-styled SJD/JSD · British-styled Ph.D. in Law · Substantially above a Ph.D. · Scholarly publications · Authority · Bologna process · Tenure · Affirmative action

4.1 Introduction

People like to ask what qualification comes after you obtain a Ph.D. In this chapter, we will examine this question, focusing on postdoctoral studies in law. In Chap. 3, we examined the concept of a British-styled law doctorate as it obtains in the UK, the Commonwealth and other pertinent jurisdictions, maintaining that while most Commonwealth countries generally have a common approach to the concept and structure of a doctoral degree in law, the practice in the US is somewhat different. We posited that the point of a doctorate is that it recognizes an independent contribution to the subject rather than taught coursework, however advanced.

In this chapter, we maintain the same thesis, that, is, regarding the difference between a British-styled Ph.D. in Law, on the one hand, and the American-styled JD, SJD and JSD programs, on the other. At the outset, it should be made clear that university appointments or job titles such as lectureships, readerships and professorships are not academic qualifications. Rather, they are faculty positions to which you get appointed or promoted. Indeed, a Ph.D. degree, for example, can be obtained before or after one is appointed or promoted to any of these job titles. Nobody

K. K. Mwenda, *Doctoral Degree Programs in Law*,
SpringerBriefs in Law, https://doi.org/10.1007/978-3-030-88421-5_4

ever studies for a qualification known as ‘lecturer’, ‘reader’ or ‘professor’, notwithstanding the variations in the nomenclature between faculty positions in the UK and the US. In both the UK and the US, you can become a full professor of law, and even hold a professorial chair, with only a first professional law degree, that is, the LLB in the case of the UK, and the JD in the case of the US, if you can demonstrate thought leadership through published scholarly work as a leading academic over the years. To put it in context, a good analogy here is the vocation of priesthood in the Catholic Church. Once you graduate from seminary and are ordained as a priest, you can rise through the ranks to become a bishop, archbishop, cardinal and pope, respectively. But, none of these clerical positions are academic qualifications. Your qualifications are the degrees you got from seminary or university, not your appointment as bishop or such other clerical title.

And so, whether you are an academic in the UK or the US, at no time did you graduate from law school or university with a degree called ‘lecturer’, ‘assistant professor’, ‘associate professor’, ‘reader’, ‘professor’ or ‘chair’. Thus, in this chapter, we will not look at faculty positions or academic appointments since they are not academic qualifications and thus fall outside the scope of the study. By parity of reasoning, we will not examine the topic of postdoctoral fellowships in law since they, too, are not academic qualifications, but academic appointments. So, what qualification then lies beyond a Ph.D.? Or, put simply, as Whitehead observes:

> Now that Ph.D.’s are becoming more commonplace, and that there are increasingly more routes to obtain one e.g. traditional, educational (taught), professional (clinical), Ph.D. by publication/portfolio etc., is there a point whereby we might consider the ‘next level’ of qualification?[1]

4.2 The Concept of a Higher Doctorate

Whereas a freshly graduated Ph.D. holder can pursue opportunities for a postdoctoral fellowship or get appointed as an Assistant Professor of Law (or its equivalent, the post of ‘Lecturer in Law’ in some British universities), pursuing a higher doctorate in law is never the immediate step after a Ph.D.. It should be noted that the concept of an earned higher doctorate that is very significantly higher than a Ph.D. is one that is rare in the US and Canada, but more established in the UK, Ireland and other Commonwealth countries.[2] Higher doctorates, it should be emphasized, are very rarely awarded. They are reserved for those senior scholars that have made exceedingly significant contributions to a science or body of knowledge through exceptionally insightful and distinctive scholarly publications, earning them recognition as international authorities in the field of research that forms the basis of the degree.

---

[1] D. Whitehead (2013), What will be the next qualification after a Ph.D.?

[2] A higher doctorate should not be confused with an honorary doctorate, although both awards carry similar names of the degree actually awarded (e.g. Doctor of Laws, Doctor of Letters, Doctor of Science, Doctor of Civil Law, and so forth). A higher doctorate, it should be emphasized, is an earned award, but an honorary doctorate is not.

In most cases, where a higher doctorate is conferred, the recipient, often a senior professor, is almost at the end of his or her academic career or is even retired. Even so, not many senior law professors ever receive a higher doctorate. As one senior law professor whispered to me when I was receiving my first higher doctorate:

> The main reason why most of us don't apply for this degree is that if, as a senior professor, you submit the required substantial body of your published scholarly work for examination for a higher doctorate by a distinguished panel of examiners who, like you, are also senior professors, and the examiners reject your work or fail it, not only will the whole encounter be embarrassing and shameful, it could also take away the credibility of your professorship.[3]

Indeed, many senior law professors know the prestige of being awarded a higher doctorate in academia, but choose willfully to shut their eyes to the obvious, dreading the possible outcome that could ensue should they ever attempt, especially if one has not built a credible portfolio of sole authored scholarly work, as opposed to a collection of edited volumes of conference proceedings or books that are mainly co-authored. Others have simply been compiling cases, statutes and other legal materials over the years into some form of compendium or books.

In her study of higher doctorates in the UK, Barnes posits that appointing examiners could be challenging for higher doctorates and that, despite internal screening, not all applications for a high doctorate are successful.[4] Such issues often bring about insecurities in some senior academics who would want to apply for a higher doctorate. Also, some examiners of higher doctorates tend to be uncomfortable with the idea of examining an academic peer such that the examination process can be slow and tedious, possibly because of the issue of disliking the prospect of not recommending a peer for the award.[5]

The hesitation of many senior professors to apply for a higher doctorate occurs in various schools, faculties or academic departments.[6] For example, it is not uncommon to find a law professor comforting himself that, after all, he has examined a higher doctorate before or that as long as one holds a Ph.D. there is hardly any difference between a Ph.D. and a higher doctorate.[7] But such polemics are not free from illogical difficulties.[8] Research shows that the common criteria at many UK universities for the submission of published work for a higher doctorate, as listed in the order of ranking, are as follows:

---

[3] The name of the concerned senior law professor is withheld here since the conversation took place in camera. The said senior professor's view explains why there are extremely few higher doctorate degree holders in many Commonwealth countries. For example, the entire English-speaking Africa has arguably not more than ten (10) higher doctorate degree holders in law.

[4] T. Barnes (2013), p. 15.

[5] See Ibid., p. 15.

[6] See Ibid., 17.

[7] Discussions with some law professors in various Commonwealth countries over a period of ten years between 2010 and 2020.

[8] See the explanation in Ibid.

(a) Work of high distinction which constitutes an original, sustained and significant contribution to the advancement of knowledge (or scholarship) or the application of knowledge through research;
(b) Original (published) work of distinction/high impact journals;
(c) Leading *international* authority in the field of study concerned;
(d) Original research over a 'sustained period', e.g., not less than seven years;
(e) Distinguished, substantial and original contributions to advancements in *learning*;
(f) Leading authority in the field of study; and/or
(g) Substantial quantity (as well as quality) of publications.[9]

Powell and Crouch posit that "a higher doctorate is an award that is at a level above the initial doctorate (*e.g.* the Ph.D.) and that is typically gained not through a defined programme of study but rather by submission of a substantial body of research based work."[10] Examples of higher doctorates include the Doctor of Divinity (DD), Doctor of Civil Law (DCL), Doctor of Laws (LLD), Doctor of Science (DSc), Doctor of Music (DMus), Doctor of Social Sciences (DSocSc), Doctor of Science in Economics (DSc(Econ)), Doctor of Medicine (MD), and Doctor of Letters (DLitt) degrees found in the UK, Ireland and some Commonwealth countries.[11] As noted above, these degrees are sometimes conferred as honorary doctorates, that is, where they are awarded not as an 'earned' degree, but an honorific, especially in the US where there is no concept of a higher doctorate.[12]

It is important to observe that within the Commonwealth, some universities refer to higher doctorates as senior doctorates.[13] In South Africa and Wales, for example, the few universities that offer higher doctorates in law refer to them as senior doctorates.[14] To illustrate, South Africa's University of Witwatersrand offers a Ph.D. in Law program and the rarely awarded senior doctorate degree of Doctor of Laws (LLD).[15] Also, Rhodes University in South Africa has a similar structure of the Ph.D. in Law program and the rarely awarded senior doctorate degree of LLD.[16] Rhodes University postulates that:

> A senior doctorate from Rhodes University may be awarded to a scholar of international stature whose published works constitute a distinguished contribution to the advancement of knowledge in a field falling within the scope of the studies represented in the University. Such distinguished contribution will normally have resulted in the candidate having established a long-held and substantial international reputation in the field.[17]

---

[9] See T. Barnes (2013), p. 11.

[10] S. Powell and N. Crouch (2008), p. 9.

[11] See Ibid., pp. 10–12.

[12] Ibid, p. 14.

[13] See below.

[14] See below.

[15] University of Witwatersrand (2019), p. 15.

[16] See below.

[17] Rhodes University (2016), p. 33.

Closely related to this, the University of Cape Town in South Africa maintains a Ph.D. in Law program and the rarely awarded senior doctorate degree of LLD, arguing that:

> The Degree of Doctor of Laws may be obtained for a substantial body of work that has already been published. Such work must constitute an original contribution to, or an important advance on, knowledge in the subject. This degree is the senior doctorate in the Faculty of Law. It is awarded rarely, as a mark of respect, normally only for work undertaken over a period of many years which has established the candidate as the leading authority in his or her field.[18]

In Wales, Cardiff University and Swansea University also refer to their higher doctorates as senior doctorates.[19] Thus, the nomenclature in South Africa and Wales are the same. So, what is the difference between a Ph.D. and a higher or senior doctorate?

4.2.1 The Difference Between a Ph.D. and a Higher or Senior Doctorate

Contrasting a higher or senior doctorate from a Ph.D., Powell and Crouch submit that, "Therefore, where a Ph.D. has come to indicate mastery of a narrow field (narrow in the sense of representing possibly three years of research study only) the higher doctorate may be seen as indicating command over a field of study and a sustained contribution to understanding within that field."[20] In Chap. 3, we looked at the concept of Ph.D. by publication. Both the Ph.D. by publication and the higher doctorate involve the submission of a portfolio of published work. So, what is the difference between the two?

In Chap. 3, we observed that a Ph.D. by publication (i.e. published work), although involving the submission of a portfolio of published work, is assessed at the same standard as a Ph.D. by thesis. We also noted that a Ph.D. by publication should not be confused with a higher or senior doctorate and that the Ph.D. by publication is similar to the writing of three separate articles, each of significant length and capable of being the lead article in a US law review, for the JSD or SJD degree. In the UK, as noted in Chap. 3, a minimum of five to eight published pieces are required, but this varies between institutions and depends on their length. So, both the UK and the US have versions of a doctoral degree in law by published work, although the US-styled SJD or JSD will also involve some taught coursework, at least, in the first year. As the University of Chester in the UK observes:

---

[18] University of Cape Town Faculty of Law, Department of Public Law (Online), "Doctoral degrees—Doctor of Law (LLD)".

[19] See Cardiff University (Online), "Senior Doctoral Awards." See also Swansea University (Online), "Guide to the degree of senior doctorate.".

[20] S. Powell and N. Crouch (2008), p. 9.

Fig. 4.1 A general pecking order from Ph.D. to higher doctorate

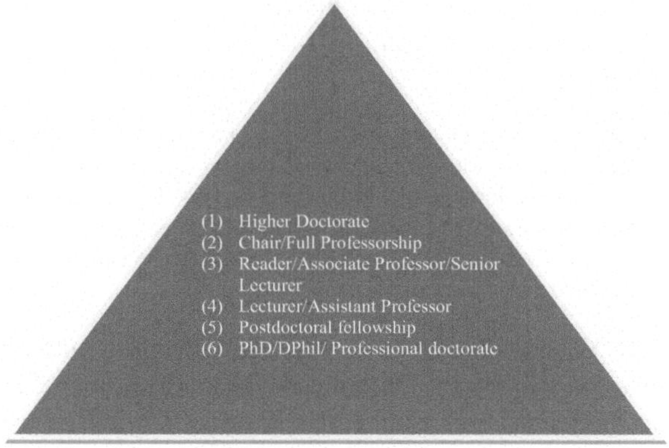

> The Higher Doctorate degree differs from the Ph.D. degree in several ways: the Ph.D. is awarded for sustained work on a single project over a relatively short period of years (typically three or four). Similarly, it is different from the Professional Doctorate, which is equivalent to the Ph.D., but normally includes a certain amount of taught material, plus case studies based on the candidate's high-level work in their employment.[21]

Indeed, a higher doctorate is *substantially* higher than a Ph.D. in Law or an JSD or SJD, notwithstanding that the Ph.D. or JSD/SJD was obtained by published work.[22] Figure 4.1 helps to put things in perspective.

There are also cases where a professor who has no Ph.D., but only a first degree and a masters degree, might be interested in getting a higher doctorate or a Ph.D. by published work. Also, some Associate Professors or Senior Lecturers can, if they have sufficient scholarly depth through demonstrable scholarly publications, apply to be admitted to a Higher Doctorate. In both cases, depending on the level and depth of the applicant's published work, the professor or associate professor can go for either a higher doctorate or a Ph.D. by published work.[23] In most cases, a higher doctorate is a form of a *lifetime achievement award*.[24] It stands at the pinnacle of authoritative scholarly work of international repute. As the University of Warwick Business School points out:

> Higher doctorates, a form of 'lifetime achievement award', are awarded to academics who have shown a considerable, original, and sustained contribution to their field of scholarship at the very highest international level. It involves the consideration of the candidate's peer-reviewed research by external assessors who are themselves of the highest academic distinction, who then make a recommendation to the University as to whether the higher doctorate should be awarded.[25]

---

[21] University of Chester (Online), "Local Professor 'Excells' to achieve First Higher Doctorate Degree: The University awarded its first Higher Doctorate degree at its graduation ceremony in March to the appropriately named Professor Peter Excell.".

[22] See generally, S. Powell and N. Crouch (2008).

[23] However, some universities such as the University of Oxford do not offer a Ph.D. by published work, though they offer higher doctorates. See the University of Oxford (Online), "Higher Doctorates.".

[24] See below.

[25] See the University of Warwick, Warwick Business School (2012), Dean of Warwick Business School awarded higher doctorate.

In general, an application for a higher doctorate often involves the submission of dozens of lead articles and/or several scholarly books for examination. The portfolio of published work submitted for a higher or senior doctorate can be huge enough to fill two medium-size carton boxes. The submission should evidence the level and depth of the applicant's published scholarly work over his or her lifetime.[26] As already established above, a higher doctorate is never the immediate step after a Ph.D.

It is important to point out that a prospective applicant for a higher doctorate who has no Ph.D. or SJD/JSD degree can be considered eligible to apply for a higher doctorate at many universities in the Commonwealth if such applicant can show that he or she is an established authority of international repute with a substantial body of published scholarly work.[27] Some universities add that the applicant must be a graduate of the university where he or she is seeking the higher doctorate or be a member of the academic staff of that university.[28] Other universities permit individuals from outside the university with a longstanding working relationship with that university to apply.[29] Then, there are also certain universities that accept applications from any applicant as long as he or she meets the high threshold scholarly distinction.[30] And so, it is not uncommon for a senior professor who holds a bachelors or masters degree, as the highest qualification, to apply for a higher doctorate to cover up for the missed opportunity of the Ph.D.

Some universities in continental Europe have various versions of postdoctoral degrees that somewhat try to mirror the concept of a higher doctorate in the UK, Ireland and other Commonwealth countries, but most of those continental European awards are a lighter version of a real higher doctorate.[31] For example, until 1984, many universities in France offered the Doctorat d'État (*i.e.* 'State Doctorate'), as a second doctorate, ranked at a higher level than the doctorat de troisième cycle (*i.e.* 'postgraduate doctorate').[32] In 1984, the Doctorat d'État was replaced by the Habilitation à diriger des recherches.[33] However, both the Doctorat d'État and the Habilitation could be deemed to be a lighter version of a real higher doctorate, as they often involve a second thesis pursued not long after obtaining the doctorat de troisième cycle or Ph.D., notwithstanding that this second thesis is a bit more demanding than the Ph.D. one.

Closely related to French experience, German universities also offer the Habilitation postdoctoral program.[34] The German Federal Ministry of Education and Research postulates that:

---

[26] See Ibid.

[27] See S. Powell and N. Crouch (2008), pp. 14–15.

[28] See Ibid., pp. 14–15.

[29] See Ibid., pp. 14–15.

[30] See Ibid., pp. 14–15.

[31] See below.

[32] APAC (Online), "Doctorat d'État".

[33] See Ibid.

[34] See below.

> If you would like *to become a professor at a German university*, you have to use the time after completing your doctorate to attain 'eligibility for professorship' (Berufungsfähigkeit). Depending on your subject, research focus and academic interest, this postdoctoral qualification phase can differ considerably. In a *first postdoc phase* – as a rule, two to four years after completion of a doctorate – you will gain research and, if necessary, teaching experience at a university or a non-university institute, and possibly in industry. You can also use this time to produce your own publications, engage in further training at congresses and develop your soft skills. International research experience can also be gained during this period of further training and qualification.[35]

The German Federal Ministry of Education and Research continues, observing that:

> *Experienced postdocs* can then meet the requirements for appointment to a professorship with work on a habilitation treatise, a junior professorship or evidence of other academic accomplishments, such as a leadership position in a junior research group or in industry.[36]

Drawing a distinction between the German Habilitation award and the Habilitation awards in other parts of continental Europe, Barnes argues that the German Habilitation,

> Despite having some equivalence with the 'Habilitation' post-doctoral awards available in some parts of Europe, it also has some significant differences. A Habilitation degree in Germany, for example, formally determines whether a person is sufficiently suited as a scholar and a teacher to be a university professor in a specific field. Assessment is based on a professorial thesis (or Habilitation thesis), or a body of academic publications submitted by the candidate for review by an academic committee – the award exceeds that of a Ph.D. in that the research must be based on independent scholarship, and the candidate may also be required to document their lecturing activity at a scientific university in a subject relevant to the postdoctoral university degree (Freie Universitat Berlin, 2012; LMU Munich, 2012).[37]

Barnes proceeds to draw a distinction between the objectives of the continental European Habilitation award and those of a UK-styled higher doctorate, postulating that,

> In the UK by contrast, the purpose of the higher doctorate is less to qualify the candidate for academic activity as to recognise a substantial and distinguished contribution in original research over a significant period of time, and/or to facilitate promotion to professorial level. As such, the DSc may be sought at the mid-career stage (for promotion purposes) whilst the DLitt is often awarded to experienced academics already in possession of a professorship (QAA,2011). Thus, any similarity with the Habilitation degree is largely confined (in broad terms) to the requirement to demonstrate the research credentials of the candidate, but at differing career stages, and for quite different purposes.[38]

Other continental European countries that offer the Habilitation award include Austria, Liechtenstein, Switzerland, and Poland.[39] The Danish *doktorgrad*

[35] German Federal Ministry of Education and Research (Online), "The path to a professorship".

[36] Ibid.

[37] T. Barnes (2013), p. 6.

[38] Ibid., p. 6.

[39] As observed through study tours of these countries between 2000 and 2011.

(dr. phil.) is also considered a higher doctorate in the Denmark and is said to be the most advanced academic degree awarded in that country.[40] As the Aarhus University explains:

> The degree is normally taken by researchers who have already obtained the Ph.D. degree. The doktorgrad is thus not equivalent to the Ph.D. degree. A higher doctoral dissertation is a major work of academic writing on which the award of a higher doctoral degree is based. The award of a higher doctoral degree constitutes recognition of the fact that the author has considerable academic insight and maturity, and that the dissertation represents significant academic progress (section 3 subsection (2) of the Danish executive order on higher doctoral degrees). The dissertation is defended at an oral defence to which the public is granted access. Anyone who has acquired a Master's degree or a Ph.D. degree within the subject area concerned is entitled to submit a higher doctoral dissertation for assessment.[41]

Notwithstanding the dictates of the Danish executive order on higher doctoral degrees,[42] we submit that the Danish *doktorgrad* (dr. phil.), like the German and French equivalents discussed above, is also a lighter version of a real higher doctorate since it involves a second thesis pursued not long after obtaining the Ph.D., despite the dr.phil thesis being more demanding than the Ph.D. one. Similarly, the 'Doktor nauk' found in Russia and some former Soviet republics is another lighter version of a real higher doctorate. In these countries, the doctoral degree system has a two-tier structure and is organized as follows:

> *First doctoral degree* (Kandidat nauk 'кандидат наук', 'Candidate of Science in …')
>
> *Second doctoral degree* (Doktor nauk 'доктор наук', 'Doctor of Science in …').
>
> «In countries with a two-tier system of doctoral degrees, the *degree of Kandidat Nauk* should be considered for recognition at the level of the first doctoral degree.
>
> In countries with only one doctoral degree, the degree of Kandidat Nauk should be considered for recognition as equivalent to this degree.
>
> In countries with a two-tier system of doctoral degrees, the degree of Doktor Nauk should be considered for recognition at the level of the second doctoral degree.
>
> In countries in which only one doctoral degree exists, the degree of Doktor Nauk should be considered for recognition at the level of this degree».[43]

4.3 The Implications of the Bologna Process on the Higher Doctorate in Europe

In Chap. 3, we examined salient features of the Bologna process, stressing that the said process strives to bring more coherence to higher education systems across Europe. We observed further that under the Bologna process, all participating countries have agreed to, *inter alia*, introduce a three-cycle higher education system consisting of

---

[40] See Aarhus University (Online), "Higher Doctoral Dissertations".

[41] See Ibid.

[42] See Ibid.

[43] Kazan University (Online), "Doctoral Degree System." See also generally O. Kouptsov (1997).

bachelor's, master's and doctoral studies. Since 2003, Norway, for example, has been following the objectives of the Bologna process, implementing a "3 + 2 + 3 degree system with a Bachelor's, Masters and Ph.D. structure."[44] This 3 + 2 + 3 degree system envisaged in the Bologna process does not, however, take into the place of higher doctorates on the echelon. It simply ends at the Ph.D.-level. Thus, it would be interesting to see how the concept of a higher doctorate fits into the Bologna process or if there is a separate structure for the harmonization of higher doctorates across Europe.

Clearly, the standards of the continental European lighter versions of a higher doctorate are not the same as those of the UK higher doctorate. And other Commonwealth countries that offer the higher doctorate draw inspiration from the UK model. So, is the future of higher doctorates in the UK and continental Europe now bleak or has the UK's January 31, 2020 withdraw from the European Union saved the British higher doctorate from exclusion by the Bologna process?[45]

4.4 Significance of the Higher Doctorate

Durham University was the first university in the UK to award a higher doctorate in any field.[46] Durham awarded its first higher doctorate, a Doctor of Science (DSc), in 1882.[47] Today, several universities in the UK and other Commonwealth countries have provisions for the award of higher doctorates, although these degrees are rarely awarded.[48] In the field of law, a higher doctorate is typically referred to as the Doctor of Laws (LLD) degree at many universities in the Commonwealth.[49]

In South Africa, the LLD degree is essentially a Ph.D. in Law at many universities except at the University of Cape Town, Rhodes University and the University of Witwatersrand.[50] Unlike other South African universities, these three universities

---

[44] See Study in Norway (Online), "Higher education system".

[45] See K. Proctor and D. Boffey (2021).

[46] T. Barnes (2013), p. 6.

[47] Ibid., p. 6.

[48] See generally Ibid.

[49] See generally Ibid.

[50] See above. In the past, the website of the University of Natal Faculty of Law showed that that university also offered a Ph.D. in Law program and the senior doctorate degree of LLD. Later, after the birth of the University of KwaZulu-Natal, the updated website provided for the versions of a Ph.D. in Law and LLD found at the University of Pretoria and the University of South Africa; that is, both Ph.D. and LLD degrees ranked at Ph.D.-level. We will discuss below these versions of the University of Pretoria and the University of South Africa Ph.D. in Law and LLD. Here, suffice it to say, the current version of the website of the University of KwaZulu-Natal Faculty of Law no longer reflects these nuances and it is not even clear whether or not the university still offers an LLD. Only the Ph.D. in Law program is listed on the website of the University of KwaZulu-Natal Faculty of Law (https://law.ukzn.ac.za/postgraduate-studies/).

offer both a Ph.D. in Law and the rarely awarded senior doctorate degree of LLD.[51] An interesting departure here is the case of the University of Pretoria and the University of South Africa that both offer the Ph.D. in Law and the LLD as a Ph.D.-equivalent qualification.[52] At the University of Pretoria, a Ph.D. in Law candidate often starts as a Master of Philosophy (MPhil) in Law student before transitioning to Ph.D. status,[53] whereas an LLD candidate often starts as a Master of Laws (LLM) degree student before transitioning to LLD status.[54] Similarly, at the University of South Africa, an LLM degree holder can pursue research for the LLD degree whereas a holder of a multi- inter- and trans-disciplinary masters degree who does not have an LLM degree can pursue research for the Ph.D. in Law.[55] At the University of Cape Town, prior to the introduction of the LLD degree as a senior doctorate, the University of South Africa version of both the Ph.D. in Law and LLD obtained there too.[56] Otherwise, both the Ph.D. in Law and LLD programs at the University of Pretoria and the University of South Africa are the equivalent of a British Ph.D. in Law.

In general, the nomenclature used by many South African law schools for their 'Ph.D. in Law' program is like that found in some parts of continental Europe where a Ph.D. in Law is referred to as 'Doctor of Laws' (LLD).[57] But such an LLD is not a senior doctorate and is substantially different from the LLD offered at universities such as the University of Cape Town, Rhodes University and the University of Witwatersrand. In the UK, the University of Oxford does not refer to its higher doctorate in law as a 'Doctor of Laws' (LLD) degree. Rather, Oxford uses a different nomenclature and refers to its higher doctorate in law as the degree of Doctor of Civil Law (DCL),[58] presumably because Oxford's most prestigious masters degree in law (by coursework) is called the Bachelor of Civil Law (BCL). According to the University of Oxford,

> The degree of DCL is intended to recognise excellence in legal scholarship, broadly defined. In evaluating a DCL application, the judges will be asked to consider whether the evidence submitted by the candidate demonstrates excellence in academic scholarship and is: a. of the absolute highest quality; b. substantial in scale and in the contribution it has made to knowledge; c. sustained over time and showing current and continued contribution to scholarship; d. authoritative, being able to demonstrate impact on the work of others; e. of

---

[51] See generally explanation in, Ibid.

[52] See below.

[53] University of Pretoria (2017b) "Programme: Ph.D.".

[54] University of Pretoria (2017a), "Programme: LLD." However, it is not clear whether the special regulations for the award of an LLD degree by published work at the University of Pretoria are still in force or not. The version of an LLD awarded by published work at the University of Pretoria was essentially a Ph.D. by published work, not a higher or senior doctorate.

[55] University of South Africa (Online), "Doctoral Degrees".

[56] The University of Cape Town Faculty of Law website has since been updated to reflect the LLD as a senior doctorate, and no longer a Ph.D.-equivalent qualification.

[57] Stockholm University, for example, offers an LLD which is essentially a Ph.D. in Law. See Stockholm University (Online), "Doctoral Studies." Also, the University of Helsinki in Finland has a similar version of an LLD which is basically a Ph.D. in Law. See University of Helsinki (Online), "Apply to the Faculty of Law".

[58] See Faculty of Law, the University of Oxford (Online), "Higher Doctorates".

global reach and international importance within the field; and f. of such breadth or covering such branches of knowledge appropriate to the field and in line with disciplinary norms and expectations.[59]

By contrast, the Doctor of Civil Law degree (DCL) program offered by McGill University in Canada is not a higher doctorate, but the equivalent of a Ph.D. in Law.[60] A significant feature of the higher doctorate degree is that it is a way of providing formal public recognition to scholars who have made significant, distinguished and coherent contributions to the advancement of knowledge in their field of expertise.[61] As the University of Auckland in New Zealand observes:

> In addition to the degree of Doctor of Philosophy, the University offers higher doctorates in Engineering (DEng), Laws (LLD), Literature (LittD), and Science (DSc). These are the highest academic awards offered by the University and are awarded to graduates or close affiliates of the University of Auckland who have published original work that has, over an extensive period of time, given them authoritative standing and international eminence in their respective field. The higher doctorate is thus to be seen as recognition of real distinction in one of these areas of study. It is awarded rarely and only after rigorous examination of a substantial and significant corpus of material.[62]

In terms of the level or depth of contribution, a higher doctorate is awarded, by definition, for a contribution that can be judged to be *substantially* higher than that of a Ph.D..[63] Higher doctorates, it should be stressed, were introduced in the UK before the introduction of Ph.D.s.[64] The first Doctor of Philosophy (DPhil) in the UK was awarded by the University of Oxford in 1917,[65] along the lines of the American and German model.[66] Examining developments leading to the introduction of the DPhil program at Oxford, Marianus contends that:

> Back in the nineteenth-century, the DPhil was a higher doctorate similar to the DLitt at the ancient Scottish universities, which at that time adhered to the continental rather than the English university model. Around World War I, universities in Britain decided to introduce the concept of the Ph.D. in response to the fact that they were losing students to European and US universities who wished to do a Ph.D. there. Those students were allowed to go direct from graduation with their bachelors' degree to registration for Ph.D. at their new institution, whereas if they had stayed in Britain and sought to supplicate for DLitt or DPhil they would usually have had to wait until they were 30 until they were eligible, and then have faced a tougher examination. You could usually only be a candidate for a higher degree at the institution where you had graduated with your first degree, except for a transference arrangement (still pertaining) between Oxford, Cambridge and Trinity College Dublin.[67]

---

[59] See Ibid.

[60] See McGill University Faculty of Law (Online), "Doctoral Program".

[61] See the University of Queensland, Australia (Online), What is a higher doctorate?

[62] See the University of Auckland, New Zealand (Online), "Regulations: Higher Doctorates".

[63] See S. Powell and N. Crouch (2008), p. 28.

[64] See below.

[65] The Quality Assurance Agency for Higher Education (2011), p. 12.

[66] See generally R. Simpson (1993).

[67] D. Marianus (Online) Ph.D. and DPhil differences.

According to Marianus,

> The Ph.D. was regarded with deep suspicion by many British universities and was deliberately *not* accorded the status of the higher doctorates. At Cambridge, for example, all doctors get to wear a scarlet festal gown *except* the Ph.D., who gets a plain black gown with scarlet facings attached with safety pins. Nor do Ph.D.s achieve the precedence of other doctors within the university. Edinburgh preserved the DPhil and Ph.D. alongside each other for a few years. Now it makes absolutely no difference in Britain what the degree is called; the old-style DPhil no longer exists. At a minority of universities, the nomenclature DPhil has been adopted for the Ph.D. (Oxford, York, Sussex etc.) but there is no difference of any kind between the requirements for these degrees and for Ph.D. (thus making this distinction potentially somewhat misleading, particularly in view of the former difference in status between DPhil and Ph.D.).[68]

By contrast, the first higher doctorate degree awarded in the UK, as already established above, was by the University of Durham in 1882.[69] So, before the Ph.D. was introduced, the higher doctorate remained the ideal route to a full professorship in the UK as well as in many parts of Europe. Even today, a higher doctorate is very prestigious in academia and is rarely awarded while a Ph.D. is often seen as the minimal qualification to enter academia.[70]

4.4.1 The Higher Doctorate as a More Objective Benchmark for Full Professorship Appointments

In comparison to a higher doctorate, a Ph.D. is a junior doctorate and so are all its variants, including the SJD and JSD. It is therefore understandable that the pursuit of a junior doctorate is most suited to junior academics or those aspiring to enter academia, although others may wish, upon graduation, to go into research outside academia. But a senior or higher doctorate, for all intents and purposes, is not meant for juniors. Neither is it meant for the average academician. The statement provided above from the University of Auckland is instructive.[71] Many universities in the Commonwealth require that a candidate for a higher doctorate must be an authority of international eminence in his or her field. For example, the requirement for a higher doctorate at James Cook University in Australia stipulates that, 'candidates for the Higher Doctorate are assessed on the basis of published work judged by national and international peers as an indication of the candidate's *authoritative* standing in his/her field.'[72] At the University of Melbourne, the higher doctorate degree guidelines provide that:

> The degree of Doctor of Laws (LLD) is the highest qualification available by examination within Melbourne Law School. The work submitted for examination must be of such a

[68] See Ibid.

[69] See above.

[70] See the Quality Assurance Agency for Higher Education (2011), p. 10.

[71] See above.

[72] James Cook University (Online), "Higher Doctorate Degrees".

> standard that it makes '...a substantial and original contribution to legal scholarship and is of such standard as to give the candidate *authoritative* standing in the field of the candidate's study'.[73]

Similarly, the guidelines for the higher doctorate degree at the University of Manchester provide that:

> Candidates are required to show that they have made an original and substantial contribution to a major field of study. The published work submitted for a Higher Doctorate must demonstrate that the candidate is a leading *authority* in their field, and has been involved in major innovations and new developments in that field.[74]

At the University of Strathclyde, the higher doctorate guidelines provide as follows:

> The award of a higher doctorate is given in recognition of an outstanding contribution to learning and/or its application in an appropriate field of study. A higher doctorate is awarded only to a candidate of considerable experience, who may be recognized as a leading authority in the field of study concerned. To qualify for the award of the degree of Doctor of Science or Doctor of Letters a candidate must have made an original and distinguished contribution to learning. The published work should provide evidence that: (i) it is a substantial contribution to a major field of study over a significant period of time (ii) the candidate is a leading *authority* in the field, and where appropriate, (iii) has been involved in major innovations and new developments in that field.[75]

Indeed, even if the body of scholarly works intended for a higher doctorate was published as peer-reviewed articles in various prestigious scholarly journals or as books published, say, by a prestigious academic press, those works must undergo thorough examination by an eminent panel of distinguished professors to confirm that you are an *authority of international repute* before you can be awarded a higher doctorate. It is not enough that the published works appear in prestigious academic journals that conduct rigorous peer-review, as is often the case with promotions to full professorship. The published work submitted for a higher doctorate must go through another round of peer-review that is even more rigorous than that of getting published. Also, the level and depth expected at the higher doctorate level must be such that the published works submitted are *authoritative* and exceed *substantially* the contribution made by a candidate for a Ph.D. by published work, even though the latter also involves an examination of published work.

Apart from the signaling effect of a higher doctorate to affirm the *authoritative standing* in erudition of the degree-holder, the higher doctorate degree can be useful for the following:

(a) To avoid or cut down on the politics associated with promotions and tenure in academia, a higher doctorate can serve as a more objective benchmark and prerequisite qualification for appointment to a full professorship or chair than the not-so-clear criteria at some law schools;

---

[73] The University of Melbourne Law (Online), Doctor of Laws (LLD).

[74] The University of Manchester (2019), p. 3.

[75] University of Strathclyde (Online), Higher Doctorates: Procedures and Guidelines.

(b) To promote a culture of academic excellence and continuous learning through scientific research and publications so that Ph.D.-holders do not go to sleep soon after getting their Ph.D.;
(c) To strengthen the quality of the peer-review system pertaining to scholarly publications, especially where law students are made to serve as editors of law journals or law reviews;
(d) To establish an informal license to hold certain positions in academia once an individual has been vetted through the higher doctorate system; and,
(e) To affirm the scholarly contributions of a higher doctorate degree-holder.

To illustrate the issue of politics associated with tenure in academia, a recent media report states that renowned Harvard University philosophy and theological scholar, Prof Cornel West, has been denied tenure by that university.[76] The reports notes that:

> The renowned professor is ready to give the prestigious school his walking papers because they denied his request for tenure. This would be the second time he's left the school for unfair treatment.[77]

The report quotes Prof. West, as saying:

> If I cannot be put up for tenure, then it is clear they don't think I'm worthy of tenure. And I will go. It is once again this issue of just not putting up with being disrespected. It's sad you have to go through this again. But I wasn't raised to put up with being disrespected or tolerate disrespect. I don't try to negotiate respect.[78]

Prof. West first left Harvard University in 2002 after a dispute with then-president, Lawrence Summers, over Harvard University's responsibility to affirmative action and his scholarship. Prof. West returned to Harvard in 2017 after teaching at Princeton University in New Jersey and the Union Theological Seminary in New York, respectively. According to the recent media report,

> West is not the only professor having issues with getting tenure at the school. Last January, 100 faculty members signed a letter urging the dean of the faculty of arts and sciences, Claudine Gay, to investigate the process and its commitment to diversity and inclusion. Other Black professors have left the school over the last year and a half. Elizabeth Hinton departed for Yale University and Memorial Church minister Jonathan Walton left to become dean of Wake Forest University's School of Divinity.[79]

On March 8, 2021, the *New Times* reported that Prof Cornel West served previously as a tenured professor at Yale, Princeton and Harvard itself but left Harvard in 2002 after a public fight with Dr Lawrence Summers, the university's president at the time.[80] Today, Prof West is being denied tenure at the same university where he held

[76] K. Manns (2021), "Cornel West threatens to leave Harvard after being denied request for tenure".

[77] See Ibid.

[78] See Ibid.

[79] See Ibid.

[80] A. Hartocollis (2021), Cornel West Is Leaving Harvard After Tenure Dispute: The public intellectual and professor of African-American studies will head to Union Theological Seminary in New York.

tenure many years ago. It is against this background that we submit that requiring a superior academic award such as a Higher Doctorate, as one of the criteria for granting tenure at US universities, can minimize the politics associated with the granting of tenure in academia. Indeed, there is a high degree of subjectivity in the granting of tenure. And so, the introduction of a requirement that the holding of a Higher Doctorate be one of the criteria for granting tenure, akin to the German Habilitation award discussed earlier,[81] could lead to a more objective and measurable process of tenure award in the US. Following below are some perspectives on the future of the higher doctorate.

4.5 The Future of the Higher Doctorate

In a 2013 survey, Barnes examined what the future looks like for higher doctoral programs in the UK.[82] Her research findings show a mix of responses, with some respondents indicating that they expect an increase in the award of higher doctorates whilst others point to a possible decrease or a retention of the status quo.[83] There were also respondents who indicated concerns that appointing examiners for a higher doctorate could be a challenge in the future, given the issue alluded to earlier of some examiners not wanting to disappoint their peers and thus delaying the examination process.[84]

Ideally, for someone to be appointed as an examiner of a higher doctorate, the person himself or herself should hold such a qualification or be at the level of a higher doctorate degree-holder. For, how else will such an examiner be expected to understand the standards of a higher doctorate? In some universities, especially in the developing world where governance matters are often a challenge, this ideal should be upheld strictly since some examiners who do not have a higher doctorate may try to frustrate a candidate from getting one.[85] Some faculty members can even sit on the application for a higher doctorate just to frustrate the applicant. The submission we are making here follows the logic that to supervise a Ph.D., the supervisor himself or herself should at least hold a Ph.D. in order to understand what is involved from both the student and supervisor's perspectives. By parity of reasoning, the supervision of SJD and JSD dissertations, say, in the US, can benefit from this reasoning so that only law professors with a Ph.D. in a cognate field or an SJD/JSD should be allowed to supervise SJD and JSD students. Such an approach can help to raise the profile and standing of the US-styled SJD and JSD programs. Otherwise, how else will a

---

[81] See above.

[82] T. Barnes (2013), p. 14.

[83] See Ibid., pp. 14–15.

[84] See Ibid., p. 15.

[85] The prestige that the higher doctorate carries is likely to attract envy from many academics that have not published much and those who would not like to see others catch up with, or bypass, them. Indeed, academia is not free of politics.

supervisor who has never written a doctoral dissertation appreciate the complexities of preparing and supervising a doctoral dissertation for a successful defense? Writing a doctoral dissertation is research training by itself.

In Europe, despite the Bologna process advocating for the introduction of a three-cycle higher education system consisting of bachelor's, master's and doctoral studies, it is a truism that most versions of the lighter and real higher doctoral programs have not been abolished or restructured. Indeed, they continue to exist, as they existed prior to the Bologna process. Even universities in Commonwealth countries outside the UK and Canada have retained the category of higher doctorates.[86] For example, the University of Zambia offers a Ph.D. in Law program as well as the higher doctorate degree program of Doctor of Laws (LLD).[87] Similarly, the University of Nairobi offers these programs.[88] Perhaps, with globalization and the continuing internationalization of legal educational norms, we can have hope that the European influence of the higher doctorate will eventually cross the Atlantic to reach the shores of Canada and the US, as it did when it crossed the Pacific to reach the shores of Australia and New Zealand.

4.6 Conclusion

This chapter has examined the concept of a higher doctorate as the qualification that stands *substantially* above a Ph.D. at many leading universities in the Commonwealth, except for Canadian universities. The chapter distinguished higher doctorates from a Ph.D. or postdoctoral fellowship. Also, some lighter versions of a higher doctorate were noted in continental Europe. The chapter then addressed the impact of the Bologna process on the concept of a higher doctorate. A submission was made that university appointments or job titles such as lectureships, readerships and professorships are not academic qualifications, but rather faculty positions. The

86 We have provided above examples from Australia and New Zealand.

87 See the University of Zambia School of Law (Online), "Postgraduates".

88 See the University of Nairobi (Online), "Higher Doctorate Degrees": "Those eligible for the award of a Higher Doctorate of the University of Nairobi must among other requirements be holders of the Doctor of Philosophy or Doctor of Medicine degree of the University of Nairobi or the Doctor of Philosophy degree from any other recognized university of at least five years standing... The Higher Doctorate, the regulations stipulate, shall only be awarded for the original published work such as would give a candidate *authoritative* international standing in his/her particular field of research. The application must be based wholly or substantially on original work of distinction carried out by the candidate. The term 'published' shall mean printed in a referred journal, book or monograph which shall have been made available to the public".

Some ten to twelve years ago, the websites of the University of Zimbabwe Faculty of Law, the University of Dar-es-Salaam Faculty of Law and the University of KwaZulu-Natal Faculty of Law all showed that these universities also offered both a Ph.D. in Law program and the senior doctorate degree of LLD. Today, it is not clear whether both programs are still being offered at these three universities since their updated websites no longer carry information on the higher doctorate, but only cover the Ph.D. in Law program.

chapter posited that whilst a freshly graduated Ph.D. holder can pursue opportunities for a postdoctoral fellowship or get appointed as an Assistant Professor of Law (or its equivalent, the post of 'Lecturer in Law' in some British universities), pursuing a higher doctorate in law is never the immediate step after a Ph.D..

The concept of an earned higher doctorate that is very significantly higher than a Ph.D., it was argued, is one that is rare in the US and Canada, but more established in the UK, Ireland and other Commonwealth countries. Higher doctorates, as demonstrated in the chapter, are very rarely awarded and are reserved for those senior scholars that have made exceedingly significant contributions to a science or body of knowledge through exceptionally insightful and distinctive scholarly publications, earning them recognition as international authorities in the field of research that forms the basis of the degree.

The chapter went on to examine the significance of a higher doctorate in legal academia, contending that the concept of a higher doctorate is a more objective benchmark for making faculty appointments to full professorship than the not-so-clear criteria at some law schools. It was noted further noted that, apart from the signal effect of a higher doctorate, signaling the authority in erudition of the degree-holder, the higher doctorate degree can be useful in cutting down on the politics associated with promotions and tenure in academia, promoting a culture of academic excellence and continuous learning through scientific research and publications so that Ph.D.-holders do not go to sleep soon after getting their Ph.D., strengthening the quality of the peer-review system pertaining to scholarly publications, especially where law students are made to serve as editors of law journals or law reviews, establishing an informal license to hold certain positions in academia once an individual has been vetted through the higher doctorate system, and affirming the scholarly contributions of a higher doctorate degree-holder. The chapter concluded with an examination of the future of the future of the higher doctorate, arguing that, in Europe, for example, despite the Bologna process advocating for the introduction of a three-cycle higher education system consisting of bachelor's, master's and doctoral studies, higher doctorate programs have not been abolished. Optimism was expressed that, with globalization and the continuing internationalization of legal educational norms, perhaps the European influence of the higher doctorate will eventually reach the shores of Canada and the US.

References

Aarhus University. Higher doctoral dissertations. https://medarbejdere.au.dk/en/administration/researchandtalent/talentadministration/higher-doctoral-dissertations/#:~:text=A%20Danish%20doktorgrad%20(dr.,equivalent%20to%20the%20PhD%20degree. Accessed 4 Mar 2021

APAC. Doctorat d'État. https://academiccareermaps.org/glossary/doctorat-detat#:~:text=The%20Doctorat%20d'%C3%89tat%20(literally,diriger%20des%20recherches%20since%201984. Accessed 2 Mar 2021

Barnes T (2013) Higher doctorates in the UK—2013. UK Council for Graduate Education, Lichfield

Cardiff University Senior doctoral awards. https://www.cardiff.ac.uk/public-information/policies-and-procedures/senior-doctoral-awards. Accessed 2 Mar 2021

Faculty of Law, the University of Oxford. Higher doctorates. https://www.law.ox.ac.uk/content/higher-doctorates. Accessed 15 Jan 2021

German Federal Ministry of Education and Research. The path to a professorship. https://www.research-in-germany.org/en/jobs-and-careers/info-for-postdocs-and-junior-researchers/career-paths/path-to-professorship.html. Accessed 2 Mar 2021

Hartocollis A (2021) Cornel west is leaving Harvard after tenure dispute: the public intellectual and professor of African-American studies will head to Union Theological Seminary in New York. The New Times (March 8, 2021). https://www.nytimes.com/2021/03/08/us/cornel-west-leaving-harvard-union.html. Accessed 16 Mar 2021

James Cook University. Higher doctorate degrees. https://www.jcu.edu.au/course-and-subject-handbook-2017/general-information/higher-doctorate-degrees. Accessed 4 Mar 2021

Kazan University. Doctoral degree system, (From: Guidelines for the recognition of qualifications from the European countries in the Russian Federation and of Russian qualifications in the other European countries). https://kpfu.ru/eng/academics/academic-programs/degree-programs/postgraduate-doctoral-degrees. Accessed 29 Jan 2021

Kouptsov O (1997) Mutual recognition of qualifications: the Russian Federation and Other European Countries. UNESCO, Bucharest

Manns K (2021) Cornel West threatens to leave Harvard after being denied request for tenure. Yahoo! News (Friday, February 19, 2021). https://news.yahoo.com/cornel-west-threatens-leave-harvard-201900773.html. Accessed 20 Feb 2021

Marianus D. Ph.D. and DPhil differences. DegreeInfo. https://www.degreeinfo.com/index.php?threads/phd-and-dphill-differences.9164/. Accessed 5 Mar 2021

McGill University Faculty of Law. Doctoral program. https://www.mcgill.ca/law/grad-studies/doctoral-program. Accessed 2 Feb 2021

Powell S, Crouch N (2008) Higher doctorate awards in the UK. UK Council for Graduate Education, Lichfield

Proctor K, Boffey D (2021) 'Fantastic moment': Boris Johnson signs Brexit withdrawal deal. The Guardian, (Friday, January 24, 2021). https://amp.theguardian.com/politics/2020/jan/24/sombre-eu-leaders-sign-brexit-withdrawal-agreement. Accessed 10 Feb 2021

Rhodes University (2016) A guide for masters and doctoral students at Rhodes University: higher degree guide 2016. Rhodes University, Grahamstown, South Africa

Simpson R (1993) How the Ph.D. came to Britain: a century of struggle for postgraduate education. Open University Press, Buckingham

Stockholm University. Doctoral studies. https://www.jurinst.su.se/english/education/courses-and-programmes/doctoral-studies. Accessed 1 Mar 2021

Study in Norway. Higher education system. https://www.studyinnorway.no/study-in-norway/higher-education-system. Accessed 5 Mar 2021

Swansea University. Guide to the degree of senior doctorate. https://myuni.swansea.ac.uk/academic-life/academic-regulations/research-guidance/guide-to-senior-doctorate/. Accessed 28 Jan 2021

The Quality Assurance Agency for Higher Education (2011) Doctoral degree characteristics. Quality Assurance Agency for Higher Education, Gloucester

University of Auckland, New Zealand. Regulations: higher doctorates. https://www.calendar.auckland.ac.nz/en/progreg/regulations-higher-doctorates.html. Accessed 1 Mar 2021

University of Cape Town Faculty of Law, Department of Public Law, "Doctoral degrees—Doctor of Law (LLD)." http://www.publiclaw.uct.ac.za/pbl/education/doctoraldegree. Accessed 2 Mar 2021.

University of Chester. Local Professor 'Excells' to achieve First Higher Doctorate Degree: the University awarded its first Higher doctorate degree at its graduation ceremony in March to the appropriately named Professor Peter Excell. https://www1.chester.ac.uk/news/local-professor-%E2%80%98excells%E2%80%99-achieve-first-higher-doctorate-degree. Accessed 2 Mar 2021

University of Helsinki. Apply to the Faculty of Law. https://www.helsinki.fi/en/faculty-of-law/admissions/apply-to-the-faculty-of-law. Accessed 3 Mar 2021
University of KwaZulu-Natal Faculty of Law. https://law.ukzn.ac.za/postgraduate-studies/. Accessed 6 Mar 2021
University of Manchester (2019) Guidance for higher doctorates. University of Manchester, Manchester
University of Melbourne Law. Doctor of Laws (LLD). https://law.unimelb.edu.au/study/graduate-research-degrees/doctor-of-laws. Accessed 3 Feb 2021
University of Nairobi. Higher doctorate degrees. https://www.uonbi.ac.ke/higher-doctorate-degrees. Accessed 4 Mar 2021
University of Oxford. Higher doctorates. https://www.ox.ac.uk/students/academic/higher-doctorates. Accessed 10 Jan 2021
University of Pretoria (2017a) Programme: Ph.D. Yearbook 2017. https://www.up.ac.za/yearbooks/2017/programmes/view/04260004. Accessed 1 Mar 2021
University of Pretoria (2017b) Programme: LLD. Yearbook 2017. https://www.up.ac.za/yearbooks/2017/programmes/view/04260003. Accessed 1 Mar 2021
University of Queensland, Australia. What is a higher doctorate? https://support.my.uq.edu.au/app/answers/detail/a_id/1621/~/what-is-a-higher-doctorate%3F. Accessed 1 Feb 2021
University of South Africa. Doctoral degrees. https://www.unisa.ac.za/sites/corporate/default/Apply-for-admission/Master%27s-&-doctoral-degrees/Qualifications/All-qualifications?cw_college=LAW. Accessed 14 Mar 2021
University of Strathclyde (2018) Higher doctorates: procedures and guidelines. https://www.strath.ac.uk/media/ps/cs/gmap/academicaffairs/policies/Higher_Doctorate_-_Policy_Procedure_and_Guidelines_FINAL.pdf. Accessed 12 Mar 2021
University of Warwick, Warwick Business School (2012) Dean of Warwick Business School awarded higher doctorate. WBS News. https://www.wbs.ac.uk/news/2012/07/27/Dean/of/Warwick. Accessed 2 Mar 2021
University of Witwatersrand (2019) Science: rules and syllabuses 2019. https://www.wits.ac.za/media/wits-university/students/academic-matters/documents/Science%202019%20Rules%20and%20Syllabuses.pdf. Accessed 2 Mar 2021
University of Zambia School of Law. Postgraduates. https://www.unza.zm/schools/law/programmes-postgrads. Accessed 1 Mar 2021
Whitehead D (2013) What will be the next qualification after a Ph.D.? ResearchGate. https://www.researchgate.net/post/What-will-be-the-next-qualification-after-a-PhD. Accessed 3 Mar 2021

Chapter 5
Conclusion

Abstract This chapter provides an analytically critical and integrated conclusion. It brings together the main arguments in the preceding chapters and reflects on the differences in the structure and standing of the JSD or SJD degree programs and the Ph.D. in law program. This chapter also offers perspectives on the value of a higher doctorate, as a rare qualification that stands authoritatively at the apex and pinnacle of the echelon of all doctorates.

Keywords Doctor · Recognition of qualifications · Doctor of Philosophy (Ph.D./DPhil) · Doctor of Juridical Science (SJD/JSD) · US-styled SJD · UK-styled Ph.D. in Law · Professional doctorate · Higher doctorate · Habilitation · Philippines · Germany · New Zealand · United Kingdom (UK) · United States (US) · Bologna process · Senior doctorate · Junior doctorate · Honorary doctorate

5.1 Revisiting the Genesis

As we conclude this study, it is important to bring together three key themes that serve as beacons of the underlying thesis of the study. These themes are the need to develop effective doctoral programs that can sustain the supply chain of researchers, the need to develop doctoral programs that prepare graduates effectively for employment in various sectors of society and the need to have internationally competitive doctoral programs that can allow graduates to work anywhere in the world.[1] To put the discussion in context, let us take a step back to revisit the origins of a doctorate degree.

Jones posits that:

> The use of the term 'Doctor' is claimed to have first occurred to designate the position of 'Doctor in Theology' in 1151. However, the first written use of the term 'Doctor' in the context of education, came from a letter written by Pope Innocent III in 1207, where he discusses the plight of Stephen Langton, who was the Archbishop of Canterbury at the time, and where the Pope mentions Langton's recent award of Doctor of Philosophy and Theology. Since these early beginnings, the Doctor of Philosophy (or Ph.D. from the Latin: *Philosophiae Doctor*) has changed from being a professional doctorate and serving to benefit

[1] *Cf*. Park (2007), pp. 2–3.

K. K. Mwenda, *Doctoral Degree Programs in Law*,
SpringerBriefs in Law, https://doi.org/10.1007/978-3-030-88421-5_5

the individual's profession, to being a doctorate which establishes a student as a teaching professional with academia.[2]

Jones observes further that this early version of the doctorate has evolved and that, in recent history, it has divided its focus along two paths, that is, the more contemporary form endures of the Ph.D. degree as the foundation degree for entry into university as an academic and certainly as a mandatory path towards tenure at most universities, while a second and more recent adaptation of the Ph.D., known as the professional doctorate, now occupies a comfortable and viable place in modern society.[3] The Ph.D., Jones maintains, arose as the contemporary research degree in the early nineteenth century, and Berlin University takes the credit for introducing this recent form of the Doctor of Philosophy[4].

Jones contends further that because of its emphasis on research and research training, this German variant attracted scholars from across the globe, most significantly, students from the USA.[5] According to Jones, the dual emphasis of (i) appealing to large cohorts of international students, and (ii) producing a research–focused qualification rather than a teaching award, led to the migration of this model of Ph.D. training across the world.[6] Jones submits that the movement began in the USA where the first doctorate was conferred at Yale in 1861 before the concept of a doctorate migrated to Canada, with Toronto being the first Canadian university to confer a Ph.D. in 1897.[7] As Jones observes:

> There was a great deal of resistance by British Vice Chancellors, which delayed the Ph.D.'s arrival in the UK until 1914 when Oxford University awarded its first DPhil in 1917. It then crossed to the other side of the world to reach Australia with the University Melbourne conferring its first Ph.D. in 1945. The purpose of the Ph.D. (research doctorate) was to prepare students for an academic career. The model of study can be polarized into two basic forms. The US model has students undertake advanced coursework in areas of content related to the selected field of study, followed by a short research component and dissertation which is guided by a course committee. The British (and Australian) model has its students engage in solitary research and writing for the production of a substantial monograph which is supported through the expert guidance of a principal academic supervisor who has experience in the field of study.[8]

5.2 Anchoring the Debate in the Underlying Thesis

At the beginning of Chap. 1, we submitted that this book is written against the backdrop of the recently adopted Global Convention on the Recognition of Qualifications

---

[2] See Jones (2018), p. 816.

[3] See Ibid., pp. 814–825.

[4] See Ibid., pp. 814–825.

[5] See Ibid., pp. 814–825.

[6] See Ibid., pp. 814–825.

[7] See Ibid., pp. 814–825.

[8] See Ibid., p. 817.

concerning Higher Education 2019. We also outlined the main aims of the said 2019 treaty as comprising the expansion of access to higher education around the world by facilitating international exchanges of students, teachers, researchers and job-seekers as well as the strengthening of international cooperation in higher education and the contribution to raising the quality of higher education worldwide. A question was then posed: in light of one of the aspirations of the Convention, namely, that 'the international recognition of qualifications concerning higher education will facilitate interdependent learning and knowledge development', what is a doctorate degree?

Although some law schools in Asian and Pacific countries have adopted the US-styled JSD or SJD degree program in the quest to internationalize their legal education, such programs are less likely to find soft-landing in the US where even American JSD or SJD programs struggle to find acceptance among many US legal academics. It is therefore ironical that some Asian and Pacific country law schools should be copying the American model of JSD or SJD programs that are not even well-regarded in the US. Thus, it is doubtful that the goal of internationalization through the adoption of the US-styled JSD or SJD programs is working well for a number of Asian and Pacific law schools. The US legal system is quite insular even though some foreign law schools in Asian and Pacific countries keep deluding themselves that adopting US-styled JSD or SJD degree programs will bring them closer to the US legal education system.

In nearby Canada, only the University of Toronto has adopted the US-styled SJD degree program while many other Canadian universities have retained the UK-styled Ph.D. in Law model. The model of a US-styled SJD or JSD program has somewhat failed to gain traction in the North American neighboring country of Canada. In Australia, Bond University, for example, has taken a cautious approach not to completely jump off the bandwagon of the UK-styled Ph.D. in Law model. Bond University maintains a parallel system of a Ph.D. in Law and an SJD. Even so, the SJD degree is treated more like a professional doctorate akin to a Doctor of Business Administration (DBA) degree, contrasting it with the more 'serious' academic Ph.D. in Law program. Commenting on professional doctorates, also known as applied doctorates, practitioner doctorates, or clinical doctorates, Jones observes that:

> The professional doctorate made its appearance in the United States at around the same time as the Ph.D. made its way into British universities, during the second decade of the twentieth century. Harvard was the first University to award a professional doctorate with the Doctor of Education (EdD) in 1921. Professional doctorates found their way to the UK at the end of the 1980s, and degrees such as Doctor of Engineering (DEng), Doctor of Business Administration (DBA), and Doctor of Education (EdD) became popular during this time. Commenting on the rapid rise of the professional doctorate in the UK in the 1990s, Bourner et al. note that: 'By the end of the decade, professional doctorates could be found in over three-quarters of the 'old' universities and a third of the 'new' universities and the rate of growth had not abated.'[9]

A few other Australian universities have adopted the US-styled JSD or SJD degree model, but, as established in the preceding chapters, they are not as many of them

[9] See Ibid., pp. 814–825.

as those that continue to offer the UK-styled Ph.D. in Law program. The situation is quite similar in New Zealand. By contrast, in Malta, until 2014,[10] the University of Malta used to offer the LLD degree to students who had completed three years of post-graduate studies consisting of coursework in a number of core areas of law as well as the submission of a thesis.[11] Prior to the LLD, students had to complete at least three years of pre-LLD legal studies.[12] As a 2017 report shows,

> In recent years, the law course at the University of Malta has changed from a 6-year course after which students receive their LLD (Doctor of Law) qualification, to a '4+1' – year course after which students are awarded an MAdv (Masters in Advocacy) qualification.[13]

The 2017 report provides further that,

> This was done to adhere to the EU-regulated Bologna Process, because, as the Maltese Faculty of Laws themselves had put it, the previous structure was 'archaic' and 'unnecessarily lengthy'. *Simply put;* the new regulations state that, after graduating from a law course at the University of Malta…graduates need to use MAdv, and *not* Dr, since that would be… well, illegal.[14]

In India, the University of Delhi offers a UK-styled Ph.D. in Law program[15] while the National Law School of India University offers not only a UK-styled Ph.D. in Law program,[16] but also an LLD by thesis to candidates who have taught for at least ten (10) years after obtaining their Ph.D. in Law degree or those with 'exceptional academic achievements in the field of law'.[17] This version of an LLD appears closer to the German Habilitation award that is often obtained through the submission of a written thesis after one has already completed the equivalent of a Ph.D. in Law.[18] Notably,

> Most candidates qualify for a university professorship in Germany by means of the habilitation process. Traditionally, habilitation generally includes the production of a ***habilitation treatise and an examination process*** that certifies the ability to teach in an academic subject. As a rule, this can also be achieved 'cumulatively' – in other words, through the publication of several peer-reviewed essays in prestigious specialist journals.[19]

In the Caribbean islands, the University of the West Indies offers a UK-styled Ph.D. in Law program.[20] Indeed, no JSD or SJD program is offered at any of the

---

[10] See Piscopo (Online), "Law students want to retain 'Dr' title: Changes to the law course will remove the Doctorate of Laws (LLD) title".

[11] See University of Malta, Faculty of Laws (2003).

[12] See Piscopo (Online), "Law students want to retain 'Dr' title: Changes to the law course will remove the Doctorate of Laws (LLD) title".

[13] See Malta (2017).

[14] See Ibid.

[15] Faculty of Law, University of Delhi (Online), "Ph.D. related information".

[16] National Law School of India University (Online), "Ph.D. in Law".

[17] National Law School of India University (Online), "Doctor of Laws".

[18] See below.

[19] German Federal Ministry of Education and Research (Online), "The path to a professorship: qualifications for a university professorship.

[20] University of the West Indies (Online), Cave Hill Campus, Barbados, "Law—MPhil/Ph.D."

campuses of the University of the West Indies. In the Philippines, the University of the Philippines does not offer a Ph.D. in Law or JSD/SJD program, but switched in 2007 from a UK-styled undergraduate Bachelor of Laws (LLB) to a four year graduate JD program based on the US-styled JD model.[21] As the University of the Philippines reports:

> On 31 July 2007, UP President Emerlinda R. Roman approved the Change in Degree Title from Bachelor of Laws (LLB) to Juris Doctor (JD). Applicants to the program leading to Juris Doctor (JD) are required to have satisfactorily completed in an authorized university or college a bachelor's degree in arts or science.[22]

In Africa, almost all English-speaking countries have maintained the UK-styled Ph.D. in Law program, with some exceptions in South Africa where the continental European model of calling a Ph.D. in Law an LLD is quite common. No law school offers a JSD or SJD program at any university in Africa. Interestingly, in East Africa, the University of Makerere refers to its Ph.D. in Law program as an LLD,[23] akin to the approach at some South African universities. To appreciate the significance of the discussion here, let us look at some developments in Germany where, until recently, individuals that held Ph.D.s from outside Germany were barred from calling themselves 'Dr'.[24] It was not just about the 'Dr' title, but also about the recognition of foreign doctoral qualifications in Germany. As Whitlock and Smiley report in a 2008 article,

> Americans with Ph.D.s beware: Telling people in Germany that you're a doctor could land you in jail. At least seven US citizens working as researchers in Germany have faced criminal probes in recent months for using the title 'Dr' on their business cards... They all hold doctoral degrees from elite universities back home.[25]

Whitlock and Smiley submit further that "under a little-known Nazi-era law, only people who earned Ph.D.s or medical degrees in Germany were allowed to use 'Dr' as a courtesy title."[26] According to Whitlock and Smiley, "the law was modified in 2001 to extend the privilege to degree-holders from any country in the European Union."[27] Despite this legislative change, Whitlock and Smiley maintain that "docs from the United States and anywhere else outside Europe were still forbidden to use the honorific" and that the violation of the law could attract a penalty of imprisonment for a year.[28]

A closely related article, published four years later, in April 2012, posits that:

> A Nazi-era law that could have seen New Zealand scholars jailed for using the title 'Dr' in Germany is being revoked. After years of lobbying from the Education Ministry, the German

[21] University of Philippines (Online), "Juris Doctor (JD) Program".

[22] Ibid.

[23] See Makerere University School of Law (Online), Academic Programmes: Doctor of Laws (LLD).

[24] See below.

[25] See Whitlock and Smiley (2008).

[26] See Ibid.

[27] See Ibid.

[28] See Ibid.

> Government has agreed to change legislation banning New Zealand doctoral graduates from calling themselves 'Dr' while in the country. Until this month, if a Kiwi Ph.D. holder had used the title 'Dr' before their name, they could have been imprisoned for up to a year and charged with abuse of a title.[29]

The article provides further that:

> The laws are based on legislation from 1939, when the Nazi government eyed foreign degrees with suspicion and required that non-German doctors be authorised by the Reich Ministry of Science, Education and Culture. Only people who earned doctorates of philosophy or medical degrees in Germany were allowed to use 'Dr'. The law was modified in 2001 to extend the privilege to degree-holders from any country in the European Union, and later amended to include those from the United States, Israel, Canada, Japan, and Australia.[30]

Generally, there is overwhelming evidence to suggest that the UK-styled Ph.D. in Law is more common than the JSD or SJD in much of the English-speaking world. Indeed, as established in the preceding chapters, the US lacks a mechanism such as the Bologna Process or a regional treaty for the recognition of higher education qualifications, say, in North America, in order to promote the internationalization of the JSD or SJD program. Neither is the US legal academy part of a well-coordinated international forum such as the Commonwealth Legal Education Association (CLEA) that fosters and promotes high standards of legal education in the Commonwealth. The implications of this lacuna for the US are that the UK-styled Ph.D. in Law is often treated internationally as a more 'serious' academic doctorate than its counterpart, the US-styled SJD or JSD.[31] Indeed, the concept of a law doctorate in many parts of the English-speaking world, including much of continental Europe, speaks to an independent contribution to a subject rather than taught coursework, however advanced. Because of the emphasis on taught coursework in the early stages of a JSD or SJD program, the independent contribution under such a program (*i.e.* through research) is likely to be taken not to be as substantial as that under a Ph.D. in Law program that focusses primarily on research.

Further, while some US law schools permit JSD or SJD candidates to submit three lead articles published in law reviews, in lieu of a dissertation, for the award of the JSD or SJD degree, not all JSD or SJD programs make provision for this type of arrangement. By contrast, many Ph.D. in Law programs in Commonwealth countries hardly require advanced taught coursework, although some law schools there also permit a candidate to submit published journal articles for a Ph.D. by published work. That said, the standard of such a Ph.D. is expected to be at the same standard as a Ph.D. by thesis. By parity of reasoning, one would expect that the standard of a JSD or SJD by published law review articles should also be at the same standard as a JSD or SJD dissertation. The net result here is that the award of a JSD or SJD by published work does not equal the Ph.D. in Law by published work.

---

[29] Duff (2012), "Germany goes for the doctor on our Ph.D.s".

[30] See Ibid.

[31] As evidenced from several discussions held between 1995 and 2015 with colleagues in academia across the UK, Africa and North America.

5.3 From a Junior Doctorate to a Senior Doctorate

An interesting feature of the concept of a law doctorate in Commonwealth countries is that it also includes the higher doctorate degree. As a senior doctorate degree, the higher doctorate is not easily obtained and is never the immediate step after a Ph.D.. As already established in Chap. 4, pitted against a higher doctorate, a Ph.D. is a junior doctorate. By parity of reasoning, pitted against a higher doctorate, all other variants of a doctorate, including the DPhil, SJD, JSD, Ph.D. by published work and professional doctorate, are junior doctorates. For example, while both Oxford University and McGill University offer the Doctor of Civil Law (DCL) degree, the two DCL degrees do not rank at par despite carrying the same name. The Oxford DCL is a higher doctorate whereas the McGill DCL is simply a Ph.D.. The same reasoning applies, say, to a Doctor of Laws (LLD) degree from any South African university other than Rhodes University, the University of Cape Town and the University of Witwatersrand. The LLD degree offered at the said three universities[32] are higher doctorates whereas the LLD offered at other South African universities are simply Ph.D.s. Similarly, in many parts of Europe, with the exception of the United Kingdom, the LLD degree offered at many universities there are simply Ph.D.s.

Generally, the titles of many higher doctorates can be misleading to someone who is not initiated or schooled in the nomenclature of doctoral programs in Commonwealth countries. The titles of higher doctorate are also used in Commonwealth countries and the US for the award of honorary doctorates. In fact, in the US and Canada, where no concept of higher doctorate exists, titles of higher doctorates such as the Doctor of Laws (LLD) and the Doctor of Letters (DLitt) are used when conferring honorary doctorates. In the UK and other Commonwealth countries, except for Canada, the title of LLD can be awarded either as a higher doctorate or an honorary doctorate. When awarded as an honorary doctorate, the LLD is not an earned degree and no examination is required. The recipient is simply being honored for one kind of experience or another, including philanthropy. By tradition, the recipient of an honorary doctorate is expected to add in parenthesis the term ‘Hon’ after the acronym, LLD, so as to read as follows: LLD(Hon). This appellation distinguishes an honorary doctorate from a higher doctorate (LLD). The same can be said of those South African law schools that offer the LLD as a Ph.D. in Law equivalent. That LLD should be distinguished from an LLD(Hon).

In academia, the role of a higher doctorate in recognizing the degree holder as an ‘authority’ of international repute is something that should be promoted and embraced widely to lessen down on the politics that are sometimes associated with the promotion or appointment of academic staff to senior professorships. We have seen above and in the preceding chapters how Germany, for example, emphasizes on the Habilitation award, or its equivalent, as a prerequisite for holding a full professorship. Universities or law schools in the US, the UK and other Commonwealth countries can learn from the German Habilitation model. Indeed, given the rigor in the assessment for the award of a higher doctorate, such a degree can serve as a more objective

---

[32] And arguably at the University of KwaZulu-Natal.

indicator of the scholarly standing of the degree-holder to admit him or her to a full professorship or chair.[33] The adoption of such an approach could provide faculty with a more objective and measurable standard to ascend to a full professorship or chair.

References

Duff M (2012) Germany goes for the doctor on our Ph.D.s. Stuff (April 21, 2012). http://www.stuff.co.nz/editors-picks/6783089/Germany-goes-for-the-doctor-on-our-PhDs. Accessed 5 Mar 2021

Faculty of Law, University of Delhi, Ph.D. related information. http://lawfaculty.du.ac.in/Ph.D.html. Accessed 2 Mar 2021.

German Federal Ministry of Education and Research. The path to a professorship: qualifications for a university professorship. https://www.research-in-germany.org/en/jobs-and-careers/info-for-postdocs-and-junior-researchers/career-paths/path-to-professorship.html. Accessed 10 Feb 2021

Jones M (2018) Contemporary trends in professional doctorates. Stud High Educ 43(5):814–825

Joyner J (2008) American Ph.D.s can't call selves 'Doktor' in Germany. Outside the Beltway, (March 14, 2008). https://www.outsidethebeltway.com/american_phds_cant_call_selves_doktor_in_germany/. Accessed 6 Mar 2021

Makerere University School of Law. Academic programmes: Doctor of Laws (LLD). https://law.mak.ac.ug/. Accessed 3 Mar 2021

Malta L (2017) Newly-graduated maltese lawyers can still call themselves 'Dr' (even though they technically shouldn't). Lovin Malta (October 10, 2017). https://lovinmalta.com/lifestyle/living-in-malta/newly-graduated-maltese-lawyers-can-still-call-themselves-dr-even-though-they-technically-shouldnt/. Accessed 25 Feb 2021

National Law School of India University. Doctor of Laws. https://www.nls.ac.in/programme/doctor-of-laws-lld/. Accessed 2 Mar 2021

National Law School of India University. Ph.D. in Law. https://www.nls.ac.in/programme/phd-in-law/. Accessed 2 Mar 2021

Park C (2007) Redefining the doctorate (Discussion Paper—January 2007). The Higher Education Academy, York, UK

Piscopo JJ (2014) Law students want to retain 'Dr' title: changes to the law course will remove the Doctorate of Laws (LLD) title. Malta Today (January 8, 2014). https://www.maltatoday.com.mt/news/national/32958/law-students-want-to-retain-dr-title-20140108#.YDh3_uhKg2x. Accessed 1 Mar 2021

University of Malta, Faculty of Laws (2003) Guidelines regarding LLD Thesis (October 9, 2003). https://web.archive.org/web/20090123032545/http://home.um.edu.mt/laws/courses/lld.html. Accessed 1 Mar 2021

University of Philippines. Juris Doctor (JD) program. https://law.upd.edu.ph/jd-program/. Accessed 8 Feb 2021

University of the West Indies. Cave Hill Campus, Barbados, Law—MPhil/Ph.D.. https://www.cavehill.uwi.edu/gradstudies/programmes/law/law-mphil-phd.aspx. Accessed on 2 Mar 2021.

Whitlock C, Smiley S (2008) Non-European Ph.D.s in Germany find use of 'Doktor'. Washington Post Foreign Service (Friday, March 14, 2008). https://www.washingtonpost.com/wp-dyn/content/article/2008/03/13/AR2008031304353.html. Accessed 24 Aug 2021

---

[33] *Cf*. UNESCO Recommendation on the Recognition of Studies and Qualifications in Higher Education of 1993; and, the UNESCO Recommendation concerning the Status of Higher-Education Teaching Personnel of 1997.

Annex

Global Convention on the Recognition of Qualifications Concerning Higher Education 2019

Paris, 25 November 2019

Preamble

The General Conference of the United Nations Educational, Scientific and Cultural Organization, meeting in Paris from 12 to 27 November 2019 at its 40th session,

Inspired by a common will to strengthen educational, geographical, humanitarian, cultural, scientific and socioeconomic ties between States Parties, and to enhance dialogue between regions and the sharing of their recognition instruments and practices,

Recalling the Constitution of the United Nations Educational, Scientific and Cultural Organization (UNESCO), which stipulates that "the purpose of the Organization is to contribute to peace and security by promoting collaboration among the nations through education, science and culture",

Mindful of the provisions of the Charter of the United Nations of 1945, the Universal Declaration of Human Rights of 1948, the Convention relating to the Status of Refugees of 1951 and its Protocol of 1967, the Convention relating to the Status of Stateless Persons of 1954, the UNESCO Convention against Discrimination in Education of 1960 and in particular its Article 4a, the International Covenant on Economic, Social and Cultural Rights of 1966, and the UNESCO Convention on Technical and Vocational Education of 1989,

K. K. Mwenda, *Doctoral Degree Programs in Law*,
SpringerBriefs in Law, https://doi.org/10.1007/978-3-030-88421-5

Mindful of the UNESCO Recommendation on the Recognition of Studies and Qualifications in Higher Education of 1993; the UNESCO Recommendation concerning the Status of Higher-Education Teaching Personnel of 1997; the United Nations Declaration on the Rights of Indigenous Peoples of 2007; and the UNESCO Recommendation on Science and Scientific Researchers of 2017,

Building on the UNESCO regional conventions on the recognition of qualifications concerning higher education,

Reaffirming the States Parties' responsibility to promote inclusive and equitable quality education at all levels and lifelong learning opportunities for all,

Conscious of increasing international cooperation in higher education, of the mobility of students, workers, professionals, researchers and academics, of changes in scientific research, and of the different modes, methods, developments and innovations in teaching and learning,

Considering higher education, provided by both public and private institutions, as a public good and a public responsibility, and **being aware** of the need to uphold and protect the principles of academic freedom and of the autonomy of higher-education institutions,

Convinced that the international recognition of qualifications concerning higher education will facilitate interdependent learning and knowledge development via the mobility of learners and learning, academics, scientific research and researchers, and workers and professionals and will enhance international cooperation in higher education,

Respecting the cultural diversity among the States Parties, including, inter alia, differences in educational traditions and in the values of higher education,

Desiring to respond to the need for a global convention on the recognition of qualifications concerning higher education to complement the UNESCO regional conventions on the recognition of qualifications concerning higher education, and to enhance the cohesion between them,

Convinced of the need to find common, practical and transparent solutions to improve recognition practices globally,

Convinced that this Convention will promote international mobility, as well as communication and cooperation regarding fair and transparent procedures for recognition, and quality assurance and academic integrity in higher education at a global level,

Adopts this Convention on this twenty-fifth day of November 2019.

Section I. Definition of Terms

Article I

For the purposes of this Convention, the following definitions shall apply:

Access (to Higher Education): the right provided to any individual holding a qualification to apply and be considered for admission to a level of higher education.

Admission (to Higher-Education Institutions and Programmes): the act of, or system for, allowing qualified applicants to pursue higher education at a given institution and/or in a given programme.

Applicant:

(a) an individual submitting to the competent recognition authority a qualification, partial studies, or prior learning for assessment and/or recognition; or

(b) an entity acting with consent on behalf of an individual.

Assessment: the evaluation of an applicant's qualifications, partial studies, or prior learning by a competent recognition authority engaged in the evaluation of qualifications.

Competent Authority: an individual or entity that has the authority, capacity, or legal power to perform a designated function.

Competent Recognition authority: an entity which, in accordance with the laws, regulations, policies, or practices of a State Party, assesses qualifications and/or makes decisions on the recognition of qualifications.

Constituent Units: official entities of a State Party to this Convention at the level of subnational jurisdictions, such as provinces, states, counties, or cantons, in accordance with Article XX b), Federal or Non-Unitary Constitutional Systems, of this Convention.

Cross-border Education: all modes of educational delivery which involve the movement of people, knowledge, programmes, providers and curriculum across States Parties' borders, including, but not limited to, quality-assured international joint degree programmes, cross-border higher education, transnational education, offshore education and borderless education.

Displaced Person: an individual forced to move from his or her locality or environment and occupational activities to another locality or environment.

Formal Education System: a State Party's education system, including all officially recognized entities with responsibility for education, as well as public and private education institutions at all levels recognized by a State Party's competent authorities and authorized thereby to deliver instruction and other education-related services.

Formal Learning: learning derived from activities within a structured learning setting, leading to a formal qualification, and provided by an education institution recognized by a State Party's competent authorities and authorized thereby to deliver such learning activities.

Higher Education: all types of study programmes or sets of courses of study at the post-secondary level which are recognized by the competent authorities of a State Party, or of a constituent unit thereof, as belonging to its higher-education system.

Higher-Education Institution: an establishment providing higher education and recognized by a competent authority of a State Party, or of a constituent unit thereof, as belonging to its higher-education system.

Higher-Education Programme: a post-secondary programme of study recognized by the competent authority of a State Party, or of a constituent unit thereof, as belonging to its higher-education system and the successful completion of which provides the student with a higher-education qualification.

Informal Learning: learning which occurs outside the formal education system and which results from daily life activities related to work, family, local community, or leisure International joint degree: a type of cross-border education degree; a single degree recognized and/or authorized and conferred jointly upon completion of an integrated, coordinated and jointly offered programme, by two or more higher education institutions belonging to more than one country.

Learning Outcomes: a learner's acquired knowledge and skills upon completion of a learning process.

Lifelong Learning: a process which refers to all learning activities, whether formal, non-formal, or informal, covers the entire lifespan and has the aim of improving and developing human capacities, knowledge, skills, attitudes and competencies.

Mobility: the physical or virtual movement of individuals outside their country for the purpose of studying, researching, teaching, or working.

Non-formal Learning: learning achieved within an education or training framework which places an emphasis on working life and which does not belong to the formal education system.

Non-traditional Learning Modes: formal, non-formal and informal mechanisms for the delivery of educational programmes and learning activities not primarily relying on face-to-face interaction between the educator and the learner.

Partial Recognition: the partial recognition of a full and completed qualification which cannot be fully recognized on account of the demonstration of substantial differences by a competent recognition authority.

Partial Studies: any part of a higher-education programme which has been evaluated and, while not a complete programme in itself, represents a significant acquisition of knowledge, skills, attitudes and competencies.

Prior Learning: the experience, knowledge, skills, attitudes and competencies which an individual has acquired as a result of formal, non-formal, or informal learning, assessed against a given set of learning outcomes, objectives, or standards.

Qualification:

(a) **Higher-Education Qualification**: any degree, diploma, certificate, or award issued by a competent authority and attesting the successful completion of a higher-education programme or the validation of prior learning, where applicable

(b) **Qualification Giving Access to Higher Education**: any degree, diploma, certificate, or award issued by a competent authority and attesting the successful completion of an education programme or the validation of prior learning, where applicable, and giving the holder of the qualification the right to be considered for admission to higher education.

Qualified Applicant: an individual who has fulfilled relevant criteria and is considered eligible to apply for admission to higher education.

Qualifications Framework: a system for the classification, publication and organization of quality-assured qualifications according to a set of criteria.

Quality Assurance: an ongoing process by which the quality of a higher-education system, institution, or programme is assessed by the competent authority/authorities to assure stakeholders that acceptable educational standards are continuously being maintained and enhanced.

Recognition: a formal acknowledgment by a competent recognition authority of the validity and academic level of a foreign education qualification, of partial studies, or of prior learning for the purpose of providing an applicant with outcomes including, but not limited to:

(a) the right to apply for admission to higher education; and/or

(b) the possibility to seek employment opportunities.

Region: any one of the areas identified in accordance with the UNESCO definition of regions with a view to the execution by the Organization of regional activities, namely, Africa, Arab States, Asia and the Pacific, Europe, and Latin America and the Caribbean.

Regional Recognition Conventions: the UNESCO conventions on the recognition of qualifications concerning higher education in each of the UNESCO regions, including the Convention on the Recognition of Studies, Diplomas and Degrees in Higher Education in the Arab and European States bordering on the Mediterranean.

Requirements:

(a) **General Requirements**: conditions which must be fulfilled for access to higher education, or to a given level thereof, or for the obtaining of a higher-education qualification at a given level

(b) **Specific Requirements**: conditions, in addition to the general requirements, which must be fulfilled for admission to a particular higher-education programme, or for the obtaining of a specific higher-education qualification in a particular field of study.

Substantial Differences: significant differences between the foreign qualification and the qualification of the State Party which would most likely prevent the applicant from succeeding in a desired activity, such as, but not limited to, further study, research activities, or employment opportunities.

Section II. Objectives of the Convention

Article II

Building on and enhancing the coordination, revisions and achievements of the regional recognition conventions, the objectives of this Convention are to:

1. Promote and strengthen international cooperation in higher education;

2. Support interregional initiatives, policies and innovations for international cooperation in higher education;
3. Facilitate global mobility and the achievement of merit in higher education for the mutual benefit of qualification holders, higher-education institutions, employers, and any other stakeholders of the States Parties to this Convention while understanding and respecting the diversity of the States Parties' higher-education systems;
4. Provide an inclusive global framework for the fair, transparent, consistent, coherent, timely and reliable recognition of qualifications concerning higher education;
5. Respect, uphold and protect the autonomy and diversity of higher-education institutions and systems;
6. Foster trust and confidence in the quality and reliability of qualifications through, inter alia, the promotion of integrity and ethical practices;
7. Promote a culture of quality assurance in higher-education institutions and systems, and develop the capacities necessary for ensuring reliability, consistency and complementarity in quality assurance, in qualifications frameworks and in the recognition of qualifications in order to support international mobility;
8. Promote the development, collection and sharing of accessible, up-to-date, reliable, transparent and relevant information and the dissemination of best practices among stakeholders, States Parties and regions;
9. Promote, through the recognition of qualifications, inclusive and equitable access to quality higher education and support lifelong learning opportunities for all, including refugees and displaced persons;
10. Foster globally the optimal use of human and educational resources with a view to promoting education for sustainable development, and contribute to structural, economic, technological, cultural, democratic and social development for all societies.

Section III. Basic Principles for the Recognition of Qualifications Concerning Higher Education

Article III

For the recognition of qualifications concerning higher education, this Convention establishes the following principles:

1. Individuals have the right to have their qualifications assessed for the purpose of applying for admission to higher education studies or seeking employment opportunities.
2. Recognition of qualifications should be transparent, fair, timely and non-discriminatory in accordance with the rules and regulations of each State Party, and should be affordable.
3. Recognition decisions are based on trust, clear criteria, and fair, transparent and non-discriminatory procedures, and underline the fundamental importance of equitable access to higher education as a public good which may lead to employment opportunities.
4. Recognition decisions are based on appropriate, reliable, accessible and up-to-date information on higher-education systems, institutions, programmes and quality assurance mechanisms which has been provided through the competent authorities of the States Parties, official national information centres, or similar entities.
5. Recognition decisions are made with due respect for the diversity of higher-education systems worldwide.
6. Competent recognition authorities undertaking recognition assessments shall do so in good faith, giving clear reasons for decisions, and have mechanisms for appealing recognition decisions.
7. Applicants seeking recognition of their qualifications provide adequate and accurate information and documentation on their achieved qualifications in good faith, and have the right to appeal.
8. States Parties commit to adopting measures to eradicate all forms of fraudulent practices regarding higher education qualifications by encouraging the use of contemporary technologies and networking activities among States Parties.

Section IV. Obligations of the States Parties tO the Convention

This Convention establishes the following obligations for the States Parties:

Article IV. Recognition of Qualifications Giving Access to Higher Education

1. Each State Party shall recognize, for the purposes of access to its higher-education system, the qualifications and documented or certified prior learning acquired in other States Parties which meet the general requirements for access to higher education in those States Parties, unless substantial differences can be shown between the general requirements for access in the State Party in which the qualification was obtained and those in the

State Party in which recognition of the qualification is sought. Alternatively, it shall be sufficient for a State Party to enable the holder of a qualification issued in another State Party to obtain an assessment of that qualification.

2. Qualifications acquired through recognized non-traditional learning modes which are subject to comparable quality assurance mechanisms will be assessed according to the rules and regulations of the State Party, or of the constituent unit thereof, using the same criteria as those applied to similar qualifications acquired through traditional learning modes.

3. Where a qualification gives access only to specific types of institutions or programmes of higher education in the State Party in which the qualification was obtained, each State Party shall grant holders of such qualifications access to similar specific types of institutions or programmes belonging to its higher-education system, if available, unless substantial differences can be shown.

Article V. Recognition of Higher-Education Qualifications

1. Each State Party shall recognize a higher-education qualification conferred in another State Party, unless substantial differences can be shown between the qualification for which recognition is sought and the corresponding qualification in the State Party in which recognition is sought. Alternatively, it shall be sufficient for a State Party to enable the holder of a higher-education qualification issued in another State Party to obtain an assessment of that qualification, upon the request of the holder.

2. Higher-education qualifications acquired through recognized non-traditional learning modes which are subject to comparable quality assurance mechanisms and which are considered a part of the higher-education system of a State Party will be assessed according to the rules and regulations of the State Party in which recognition is sought, or of the constituent unit thereof, using the same criteria as those applied to similar qualifications acquired through traditional learning modes.

3. Higher-education qualifications acquired through cross-border education with international joint degrees or through any other joint programme undertaken in more than one country, of which at least one is a State Party to this Convention, shall be assessed according to the rules and regulations of the State Party in which recognition is sought, or of the constituent unit thereof, using the same criteria as those applied to qualifications acquired through programmes undertaken in a single country.

4. Recognition in a State Party of a higher-education qualification issued in another State Party shall have at least one of the following outcomes:

    (a) It shall provide the holder with the right to apply for admission to further higher education under the same conditions as those applicable to holders of higher-education qualifications of the State Party in which recognition is sought; and/or

(b) It shall provide the holder with the right to use the title associated with a higher-education qualification in accordance with the laws or regulations of the State Party, or of the constituent unit thereof, in which recognition is sought.

In addition, assessment and recognition may enable qualified applicants to seek employment opportunities subject to the laws and regulations of the State Party, or of the constituent unit thereof, in which recognition is sought.

5. Where a competent recognition authority can demonstrate substantial differences between the qualification for which recognition is sought and the corresponding qualification in the State Party in which recognition is sought, the competent recognition authority shall seek to establish whether partial recognition may be granted.

6. Each State Party may make the recognition of higher-education qualifications acquired through cross-border education or through foreign educational institutions operating in its jurisdiction contingent upon specific requirements of the legislation or regulations of the State Party, or of the constituent unit thereof, or upon specific agreements concluded with the State Party of origin of such institutions.

Article VI. Recognition of Partial Studies and Prior Learning

1. Each State Party may recognize, for the purpose of the completion of a higher-education programme or the continuation of higher education studies, where appropriate, and taking into account the legislation of the States Parties regarding access, documented or certified partial studies or documented or certified prior learning acquired in another State Party, unless substantial differences can be shown between the partial studies or prior learning and the part of the higher-education programme they or it would replace in the State Party in which recognition is sought. Alternatively, it shall be sufficient for a State Party to enable an individual who has undertaken documented or certified partial studies or documented or certified prior learning in another State Party to obtain an assessment of these partial studies or this prior learning, upon the request of the individual concerned.

2. Documented or certified partial completion of higher-education programmes delivered by recognized non-traditional learning modes which are subject to comparable quality assurance mechanisms and which are considered a part of the higher-education system of a State Party shall be assessed according to the rules and regulations of the State Party, or of the constituent unit

thereof, using the same criteria as those applied to partial studies delivered by traditional learning modes.

3. Documented or certified partial completion of higher-education programmes delivered through cross-border education with international joint degrees or any other joint programme undertaken in more than one country, of which at least one is a State Party to this Convention, will be assessed according to the rules and regulations of the State Party, or of the constituent unit thereof, using the same criteria as those applied to partial studies acquired in a single country.

Article VII. Recognition of Partial Studies and Qualifications Held by Refugees and Displaced Persons

Each State Party shall take the necessary and feasible steps, within its education system and in conformity with its constitutional, legislative and regulatory provisions, to develop reasonable procedures for assessing fairly and efficiently whether refugees and displaced persons fulfil the relevant requirements for access to higher education, to further higher-education programmes, or to the seeking of employment opportunities, including in cases where partial studies, prior learning, or qualifications acquired in another country cannot be proven by documentary evidence.

Article VIII. Information for Assessment and Recognition

1. Each State Party shall establish transparent systems for the complete description of the qualifications and learning outcomes obtained in its territory.
2. Each State Party, to the extent feasible based on its constitutional, legislative and regulatory situation and structure, shall put in place an objective and reliable system for the approval, recognition and quality assurance of its higher-education institutions in order to promote confidence and trust in its higher-education system.
3. Each State Party shall establish and maintain a national information centre or similar entities to provide access to relevant, accurate and up-to-date information about its higher-education system.
4. Each State Party shall encourage the use of technologies to ensure easy access to information.
5. Each State Party shall:

   (a) Provide access to authoritative and accurate information on its higher-education systems, qualifications, quality assurance, and qualification frameworks, if applicable;

(b) Facilitate the dissemination of and access to accurate information on the other States Parties' higher-education systems, qualifications, and qualifications giving access to higher education;

(c) Give advice and information, where appropriate, on recognition matters, including criteria and procedures for the assessment of qualifications, and the development of materials for good recognition practices in accordance with the laws, regulations and policies of the State Party; and

(d) Ensure the provision, within a reasonable time, of adequate information on any institution belonging to its higher-education system, and on any programme operated by such institutions, with a view to enabling the competent authorities of other States Parties to ascertain whether the quality of the qualifications issued by these institutions justifies recognition in the State Party in which recognition is sought.

Article IX. Assessment of an Application

1. In the first instance, the responsibility for providing adequate information rests with the applicant, who shall provide such information in good faith.
2. Each State Party shall ensure that the institutions belonging to its education system provide to the extent available, upon request, within a reasonable time frame and free of charge, relevant information to the holder of a qualification or to the institution or the competent recognition authorities of the State Party in which recognition is sought.
3. Each State Party shall ensure that the body undertaking assessment for the purposes of recognition demonstrates the reasons for which an application does not fulfil requirements or demonstrates where substantial differences are identified.

Article X. Information on the Competent Recognition Authorities

1. Each State Party shall provide the depository of this Convention with official notification of the competent authorities that make decisions on recognition matters in its jurisdiction.
2. Where there are central competent recognition authorities of a State Party, they shall immediately be bound by the provisions of this Convention and shall take the necessary measures to ensure the implementation of the provisions of this Convention in the jurisdiction of said State Party.
3. Where the competence to make decisions on recognition matters lies with the constituent units, the State Party shall furnish the depository with a brief statement on its constitutional situation or structure at the time of signature or when depositing its instrument of ratification, acceptance, approval,

or accession, and on any changes thereafter. In such cases, the competent recognition authorities of the constituent units so designated shall take, to the extent feasible within the State Party's constitutional situation and structure, the necessary measures to ensure the implementation of the provisions of this Convention within the State Party's jurisdiction.

4. Where the competence to make decisions on recognition matters lies with individual higher-education institutions or other entities, each State Party or constituent unit thereof, according to its constitutional situation or structure, shall transmit the text of this Convention to these institutions or entities and shall take all the necessary steps to encourage the favourable consideration and application of its provisions.

5. The provisions of paragraphs 2, 3 and 4 of this Article shall apply, mutatis mutandis, to the obligations of the States Parties under this Convention.

Article XI. Additional Requirements for Admission to Higher-Education Programmes

1. Where admission to particular higher-education programmes is dependent on the fulfilment of specific requirements in addition to the general requirements for access, the competent authorities of the State Party concerned may impose the same specific requirements on holders of qualifications obtained in other States Parties or assess whether applicants with qualifications obtained in other States Parties fulfil the equivalent requirements.

2. Where qualifications giving access to higher education in one State Party are issued only in combination with additional qualifying examinations as a prerequisite for access, the other States Parties may make access conditional on these requirements or offer an alternative for satisfying such additional requirements within their own education systems.

3. Without prejudice to the provisions of Article IV, admission to a given higher-education institution, or to a given programme within such an institution, may be restricted or selective, according to fair and transparent regulations.

4. With respect to paragraph 3 of the present article, admission procedures shall be designed with a view to ensuring that the assessment of foreign qualifications is carried out according to the principles of transparency, fairness and non-discrimination described in Article III.

5. Without prejudice to the provisions of Article IV, admission to a given higher-education institution may be based on the condition of the demonstration by the qualification holder of sufficient competence in the language or languages of instruction of the institution concerned, or in other specified languages.

6. For the purpose of admission to higher-education programmes, each State Party may make the recognition of qualifications issued by foreign educational institutions operating in its jurisdiction contingent upon specific requirements of the legislation and regulations of the State Party or the constituent unit thereof, or upon specific agreements concluded with the State Party of origin of such institutions.

Section V. Implementation Structures and Cooperation

Article XII. Implementation Structures

The States Parties agree to implement this Convention through or in cooperation with:

1. National implementation structures;
2. Networks of national implementation structures;
3. National, regional and global organizations for accreditation, quality assurance, qualification frameworks, and recognition of qualifications;
4. The Intergovernmental Conference of the States Parties;
5. Regional recognition convention committees.

Article XIII. National Implementation Structures

1. In order to facilitate the recognition of higher-education qualifications, the States Parties undertake to implement this Convention through relevant organizations, including national information centres or similar entities.
2. Each State Party will notify the Secretariat of the Intergovernmental Conference of the States Parties of its national implementation structures and of any modification in this regard.
3. National implementation structures should form and actively participate in networks.

Article XIV. Networks of National Implementation Structures

1. Under the auspices of the Intergovernmental Conference of the States Parties, the networks shall be composed of national implementation structures of the States Parties and shall uphold and assist with the practical implementation of this Convention.
2. The networks shall provide information exchange, capacity building and technical support to the States Parties upon request.

3. The networks shall seek to strengthen the interregional cooperation under this Convention and uphold links to the Intergovernmental Conference of the States Parties.
4. States Parties may participate in existing regional networks established through the regional recognition conventions or create new networks. Participation in existing regional networks shall be subject to the agreement of the relevant regional recognition convention committees.

Article XV. The Intergovernmental Conference of the States Parties

1. An Intergovernmental Conference of the States Parties, hereinafter referred to as "the Conference", shall be established.
2. The Conference shall be composed of representatives of all States Parties to this Convention.
3. The States which are not States Parties to this Convention and the heads of the regional recognition convention committees shall be invited to participate in the meetings of the Conference as observers.
4. Representatives of relevant international and regional organizations, as well as representatives of governmental and non-governmental organizations active in the field of recognition of higher-education qualifications, may also be invited to attend meetings of the Conference as observers.
5. The Conference shall meet in ordinary sessions at least every two years. It may meet in extraordinary sessions if it so decides or at the request of at least one third of the States Parties. The Conference shall have an interim work programme concerning activities between sessions. The Conference shall submit a report at each of the ordinary sessions of the General Conference of UNESCO.
6. The Conference shall meet for the first time within two years of the entry into force of this Convention, and at that time it shall adopt its own rules of procedure.
7. The Conference shall promote the application of this Convention and shall oversee its implementation by adopting recommendations, declarations, models of good practices, or any relevant subsidiary text at the global or interregional level.
8. The Conference may adopt operational guidelines for the States Parties to this Convention, in consultation with the regional recognition convention committees.
9. The Conference shall support the follow-up of the activities relating to monitoring by and reporting to UNESCO's governing bodies with regard to the implementation of this Convention.

10. The Conference shall cooperate with the regional recognition convention committees under the auspices of UNESCO.
11. The Conference shall ensure that there is the necessary information exchange between the Conference and the regional recognition convention committees.
12. The Conference Shall Examine for Adoption the Draft Amendments to This Convention in Accordance with Article XXIII. The Amendments Adopted Shall not Undermine the Principles of Transparent, Fair, Timely and Non-Discriminatory Recognition Stated in This Convention.
13. The Secretariat of the Conference shall be provided by the Director-General of UNESCO. The Secretariat shall prepare the documentation of the Conference, draft the agenda of its meetings, and ensure the implementation of its decisions.

Section VI. Final Clauses

Article XVI. Ratification, Acceptance, or Approval by Member States

1. This Convention shall be subject to ratification, acceptance, or approval by Member States of UNESCO and the Holy See in accordance with their respective constitutional and legislative procedures.
2. The instruments of ratification, acceptance, or approval shall be deposited with the Director-General of UNESCO.

Article XVII. Accession

1. This Convention shall be open to accession by all States which are not members of UNESCO but which are Members of the United Nations and are invited by the General Conference of UNESCO to accede to it.
2. This Convention shall also be open to accession by territories which enjoy full internal self-government recognized as such by the United Nations, but which have not attained full independence in accordance with General Assembly resolution 1514 (XV), and which have competence over the matters governed by this Convention, including the competence to enter into treaties in respect of such matters.
3. The instrument of accession shall be deposited with the Director-General of UNESCO.

Article XVIII. Entry into Force

1. This Convention shall enter into force three months after the date of deposit of the twentieth instrument of ratification, acceptance, approval, or accession, but only with regard to those States Parties which have deposited their respective instruments of ratification, acceptance, approval, or accession on or before that date.
2. This Convention shall enter into force with regard to any other State Party three months after the deposit of its instrument of ratification, acceptance, approval, or accession.

Article XIX. Relationship between the States Parties to this Convention and the Parties to the Regional Recognition Conventions and to Other Treaties

1. The ratification of, acceptance of, approval of, or accession to of any of the regional recognition conventions shall not be a prerequisite for the ratification of, acceptance of, approval of, or accession to this Convention.
2. The States Parties to this Convention shall:
   (a) Foster mutual support between this Convention and the other treaties to which they are parties, particularly the regional recognition conventions; and
   (b) Take into account the relevant provisions of this Convention when interpreting and applying the regional recognition conventions to which they are parties or when entering into other international obligations.
3. Nothing in this Convention shall be interpreted as modifying the rights and obligations of the States Parties under the regional recognition conventions and any other treaties to which they are parties.
4. To ensure coherent interaction between this Convention, the regional recognition conventions, any other relevant bilateral or multilateral agreements, and any other existing or future treaty or convention to which a State Party to this Convention may be or may become a party, nothing in this Convention shall be deemed to derogate from any provisions more favourable to recognition, in particular, provisions regarding national information centres, networks and substantial differences.

Article XX. Federal or Non-Unitary Constitutional Systems

Recognizing that international agreements are equally binding on States Parties regardless of their constitutional systems, the following provisions shall apply to States Parties which have a federal or non-unitary constitutional system:

(a) With regard to the provisions of this Convention the implementation of which comes under the legal jurisdiction of the federal or central legislative power, the obligations of the federal or central Government shall be the same as for those States Parties which are not federal States;

(b) With regard to the provisions of the Convention the implementation of which comes under the jurisdiction of constituent units of a State Party, such as provinces, states, counties, or cantons, which are not obliged by the constitutional system of the federation to take legislative measures, the federal Government shall inform, as necessary, the competent authorities of the constituent units of a State Party of said provisions, with its recommendation for their adoption.

Article XXI. Denunciation

1. Any State Party to this Convention may denounce, at any time, this Convention.
2. The denunciation shall be notified by an instrument in writing deposited with the Director-General of UNESCO.
3. The denunciation shall take effect 12 months after the receipt of the instrument of denunciation. It shall in no way affect the obligations under this Convention incumbent upon the State Party denouncing the Convention until the date on which the withdrawal takes effect.
4. The denunciation of this Convention shall not have any impact with respect to:

    (a) Recognition decisions taken previously under the provisions of this Convention;

    (b) The recognition assessments still in progress under this Convention.

Article XXII. Depositary Functions

The Director-General of UNESCO, as the depositary of this Convention, shall inform the Member States of the Organization, the States not members of the Organization referred to in Article XVII, as well as the United Nations, of:

(a) The deposit of all the instruments of ratification, acceptance, approval, or accession provided for in Articles XVI and XVII;

(b) The denunciations provided for in Article XXI;

(c) The amendments to the Convention adopted in accordance with Article XXIII and the date on which the amendments come into force as proposed in accordance with Article XXIII.

Article XXIII. Amendments

1. A State Party to this Convention may, by written communication addressed to the Director-General of UNESCO, propose amendments to this Convention. The Director-General shall circulate such communication to all States Parties. If within six months of the date of dispatch of the communication, no less than one half of the States Parties to the Convention reply favourably to the request, the Director-General shall present such proposal to the next session of the Intergovernmental Conference of the States Parties for discussion and possible adoption.
2. Amendments shall be adopted by a two-thirds majority of States Parties present and voting.
3. Once adopted, amendments to this Convention shall be submitted to the States Parties for ratification, acceptance, approval, or accession.
4. For States Parties which have ratified, accepted, approved, or acceded to them, amendments to this Convention shall enter into force three months after the deposit by two thirds of the States Parties of the instruments referred to in paragraph 3 of this Article. Thereafter, for each State Party which ratifies, accepts, approves, or accedes to an amendment, said amendment shall enter into force three months after the date on which that State Party has deposited its instrument of ratification, acceptance, approval, or accession.
5. A State which becomes a State Party to this Convention after the entry into force of amendments in conformity with paragraph 4 of this Article shall, failing an expression of different intention, be considered to be:
   (a) A State Party to this Convention as so amended; and
   (b) A State Party to the unamended Convention in relation to any State Party not bound by the amendments.

Article XXIV. Registration with the United Nations

In conformity with Article 102 of the Charter of the United Nations, this Convention shall be registered with the Secretariat of the United Nations at the request of the Director-General of UNESCO.

Article XXV. Authoritative Texts

This Convention has been drawn up in Arabic, Chinese, English, French, Russian and Spanish, all six texts being equally authoritative.

Depositary
UNESCO.

Entry into Force

In accordance with the terms of its Article XVIII, the Convention shall enter into force three months after the date of deposit of the twentieth instrument of ratification, acceptance, approval, or accession, but only with regard to those States Parties which have deposited their respective instruments of ratification, acceptance, approval, or accession on or before that date.

Authoritative Texts

Arabic, Chinese, English, French, Russian and Spanish.

Index

K. K. Mwenda, *Doctoral Degree Programs in Law*,
SpringerBriefs in Law, https://doi.org/10.1007/978-3-030-88421-5

The manufacturer's authorised representative in the EU is Springer Nature Customer Service Centre GmbH, Europaplatz 3, 69115 Heidelberg, Germany. If you have any concerns regarding our products, please contact ProductSafety@springernature.com

Printed and bound by CPI Group (UK) Ltd, Croydon, CR0 4YY
22/09/2026
02220945-0017